Also by C.A. Love

RUSHING INTO OBLIVION.......
The United States of America

No Wimps in Heaven!

by

C.A. Love

authorHOUSE®

AuthorHouse™
1663 Liberty Drive
Bloomington, IN 47403
www.authorhouse.com
Phone: 1-800-839-8640

First published by AuthorHouse   11/22/2009

ISBN: 978-1-4490-4362-9 (e)
ISBN: 978-1-4490-4363-6 (sc)

Library of Congress Control Number: 2009911495

Printed in the United States of America
Bloomington, Indiana

This book is printed on acid-free paper.

This book is dedicated to true
believers everywhere

"For they have sown the wind, and they shall reap the whirlwind......."

Hosea 8:7

"Be not deceived; God is not mocked: for whatsoever a man soweth, that shall he also reap."

Galatians 6:7

"Whereas it is the duty of all nations to acknowledge the providence of Almighty God, to obey His will, to be grateful for His benefits, and humbly implore His protection and favor......."

George Washington,
Thanksgiving Proclamation,
October, 3, 1789

Contents

Introduction

This book has been written for the purpose of refuting the idea that going to church, believing, and living according to Biblical teaching is for wimps and losers. That it is not a crutch to do these things, but rather a mandate from our Creator in order to obtain everlasting life.

The author attempts to point out the fallacy of the claim that God does not exist, or that there are many Gods, so just take your pick, it doesn't matter.

He also writes of choices people make that determine their eternal destination. What real courage consists of, in spite of ridicule and condemnation. He brings out the fact that, in the United States of America, those who believe in the true God of the Bible are viciously maligned as never before in our history.

Most importantly, this writer makes the distinction between "religion" and "Christianity." As you read this book, you will see that there is a vast difference.

God, or a "all-powerful deity" has been in the mind of mankind from the beginning of time because we are "created" beings; regardless of false evolutionary teaching.

That being said, this book has much food for thought. For those who believe in God, or for those who refuse to believe.

However, sooner or later in life, everyone WILL choose their eternal destiny. And it is entirely a matter of personal choice.

Finally, the author introduces the one who reads this book, to a God who is so loving and caring that He would provide a way to *everlasting life*, to *all* who would accept this marvelous gift!

Chapter One

The Meaning Of Words

Where to begin? As I have been doing research for material to write this book, that simple little question became very relevant

Just how do I go about trying to explain the meaning of the title, "No wimps In Heaven"?

First, we have to define the meaning of the term "wimp," and all of it's implications. The dictionary definition of this little word is: "A weak, ineffectual, or insipid person."

For further clarification we will ponder the significance of the three words implied by the derogatory word, "wimp."

First of all, it denotes "weakness." Now this is a word with a great variety of meaning. The broadest application is inferiority of physical, mental, or moral strength; to be pitiable or ineffective, to be easily broken or shattered.

Secondly, it indicates that a person is "ineffective." Not capable of performing satisfactorily; incompetent and inefficient.

Thirdly, it is a sign of being "insipid." This is one who is without flavor, or tasteless. Not exciting or interesting; dull and lifeless.

It is very important that we remember the meaning of these words as we view the lives of different people.

But first there are three more little words I will enter into this dialogue for your consideration and debate. And they are, "ignorant," "loser," and "stupid."

"Ignorant" is a word that most of us are familiar with. It simply means having very little knowledge, education, or experience. Lacking in a particular area or matter; heedless or unawareness.

"Loser" is a word that is used a lot to define certain types of individuals. It means one that seems doomed to lose. Someone that is unsuccessful and is unable to win, gain or take advantage; to become bewildered.

"Stupid" is another word that we hear repeatedly. It is a word that is beyond being "ignorant." The meaning is a lack of normal intelligence or understanding; slow -witted or dull, foolish, irrational, boring and tiresome. It is used as a generalized term of disapproval.

All of these words are used in a derogatory manner to disparage and belittle others that fail to meet the "standards" of our elite populace.

I will not mention the words that are filthy, nasty, indecent and obscene, because they are disgusting and not fit to print.

The point I want to make is this: these are terms used to put down and denigrate a certain class or group of people. Words that are meant to harm and destroy, not only a persons character and integrity, but an entire belief system.

Hatred is a word that I don't like to use, but indications are pointing in that direction, and is the reason for this expose. My next statement will be clear and to the point. There is a certain class of people in this country who are bound and determined to destroy another class of people that they do not agree with.

Now the use of words can be uplifting or damaging, according to the intent of the user. Malicious name calling can, and does at times, lead to physical violence and abuse. Character assassination and bodily harm can be the result of words used in an intentional and spiteful manner against another person or group of people.

Words have a very profound effect, whether they are spoken or written, once they are released into the public domain they cannot be retrieved or undone. Many times I have said things without first thinking, but once uttered I had to live with the consequences. There is an old saying that "talk is cheap," but often there is a heavy price to pay for what we say. I have heard many people speak their opinions and make verbal blunders, only to have it come back and embarrass them later on. Many times when we speak in condemnation, or ridicule others, we do so without thinking and without fact or evidence to back up what we say. Often, people will make up false accusations and lie simply to hurt someone, or put down anything they do not agree with. Slanderous words and hate speech have become very prevalent in this country. Not only in the general public, but by our esteemed leaders and many well known individuals. Such as movie "stars," other entertainment people, talk show hosts, both radio and TV personalities, also newspaper pundits.

These folks have a bully-pulpit to spew their hatred and derogatory remarks into the ears and minds of many uninformed and impressionable people who are easily and emotionally influenced by this type of rhetoric.

This all has to do with freedom of speech, right? Guaranteed under our Constitution, right again? Reality does not confirm this to be altogether factual; it all depends on what is being said and by who is saying it. Once again I will remind you that we are talking about "words." Some words promote hatred and lying, while others espouse love and truth. One would think that to advocate the truth and what is good, uplifting and righteous is a very noble and positive thing to do. However, this has it's bounds and is not popular with many of our great thinkers and secular humanistic ideologists.

There is a growing number of elitist mental midgets that would put a stop to certain words and decent speech if they could. How can this be, you may ask? Well let's get down to the nitty-gritty and open up a can of worms, shall we? It is time that some of these left-wing deviants were exposed anyway!

By this time you may have an idea as to where I am going with all of this rhetorical elaboration about "words." In some circles Christianity is regarded as a fringe group, to be castigated, maligned and done away with; not given any credibility or opportunity to exercise our freedom of speech.

Because we are discussing "words," it is absolutely necessary that we consult with The Word of God, to get His take on this subject ; I am referring to Holy Scripture. For me, this is the highest authority on any matter, bar none!

Having read and studied the Bible for many years, I am still amazed at how fresh and relevant Scripture is for the present time. As I was doing research for this book, I could not help but marvel at the incredible truth and greatness of God's Word, even though many of these passages of Scripture have been read multiple times. Praise be to His name! I cannot fully mentally grasp all that God has to say about words, our tongue and our speech. Words, and how we understand them are crucial to our existence and how we live. Understandably, this is an extreme statement and

I will attempt to make it clear as we proceed with this discussion.

One more thing I would like to make very clear at this juncture. Not everyone who claims the title of "Christian" is a true follower of Christ. Just like anything else that is for real, there can be a counterfeit. Sad to say, but there are many who claim the distinction of being a "Christian," yet haven't a clue what this really entails. We will go into some detail on this matter later on.

Now we will review some Biblical terminology and instruction; both Old and New Testament. Psalm 34:13, "Keep thy tongue from evil, and thy lips from speaking guile." In other words, don't say things that are evil, with a sly and crafty cunningness, to defame and hurt others. It doesn't take a great deal of intellectual prowess to figure this out.

The next few verses of Scripture are very telling and get into the basis of this segment of our discourse. The book of James, chapter 3, verses 5 through 8, "Even so the tongue is a little member, and boasteth great things. Behold, how great a matter a little fire kindleth!" 6-"And the tongue is a fire, a world of iniquity: so is the tongue among our members, that it defileth the whole body, and setteth on fire the course of nature; and it is set on fire of hell." 7- "For every kind of beasts, and of birds, and of serpents, and of things in the sea, is tamed, and hath been tamed of mankind:" 8- "But the tongue can no man tame; it is an unruly evil, full of deadly poison."

A very straightforward picture of the power of words and the harm they can produce. Isn't it strange that every manner of wild creature can be tamed by man, but he cannot control his own tongue? However, the place to begin is to keep our tongue from evil; which includes lying, slandering, and any words that are hurtful.

This brings us into a very sticky little issue that must be brought up to clear away any misconceptions we may have. That little point of contention is called "truth." The old saying is, "truth hurts some times." This type of "hurt" is not what the Bible speaks of as being harmful, unless it applies to the perpetrator and that could be a good thing, Except in this case it is called "justice." Anyway, I believe you get the point, that the words from our tongue can do great mischief and damage, be it intentional or even unintentional.

The last part of the 8th verse about the tongue, that it is an "unruly evil, full of deadly poison," gives us an idea of just how powerful words can be. Take note of all the riots that occur around the world and you will get a picture of the fire that words can ignite. Many of these incidents have deadly consequences.

For further understanding, we will read in Proverbs, chapter 18, verse 21, "Death and life are in the power of the tongue: and they that love it shall eat the fruit thereof." The first part of this verse is abundantly clear, but for more clarification of it's entire meaning I will give three more Scripture verses for your consideration. Proverbs 12:13, "The wicked is snared by the transgression of his lips: but the just shall come out of trouble." Transgression is construed as meaning sin or a breach of the law. Matthew 12:37, "For by thy words thou shalt be justified, and by thy words thou shalt be condemned." This is plain enough, depending upon the meaning or intent of the words we speak, either for our condemnation or our justification. Now to sum this up, let's read Second Peter 2:9, "The Lord knoweth how to deliver the godly out of temptations, and to reserve the unjust unto the day of judgment to be punished." This is very clear and concise!

So the question arises, if a man cannot control his tongue, how do we solve this problem? Would you believe that God has the answer to this also? In the book of Mark, chapter 10, verse 27, we are told this: "And Jesus looking upon them saith, with men it is impossible, but not with God: for with God all things are possible." However, we are held responsible to know "how" this works because it does not come naturally. Now this is what separates the genuine Christian from the phony, or counterfeit. Just because the Bible tells us that "all things are possible with God" does not mean we have a blank check, as a Christian, to expect God to do things that are contrary to His Word. This simply will not happen because God is a God of righteousness, and if this is not our motive also, our requests will be in vain.

For starters, we will go back to our "road map" for directions. Psalm 19, verse 14, "Let the words of my mouth, and the meditation of my heart, be <u>acceptable</u> in thy sight, O Lord, my strength, and my redeemer." This is the beginning of the "how' process of learning to control that small, unruly member of our body, the tongue. The words that we speak and the things we meditate on, or think about, <u>must be acceptable</u> to God. He is not interested in the frivolous or unseemly things that man may perceive, say, or do. Am I suggesting that God is exact and precise in how He wants us to think, speak, and act? Yes, absolutely! As a Christian, and that is who I am addressing at this point, God has clear and unequivocal requirements that we <u>must</u> abide by if we are to retain this title. God is unchangeable in His directions!

Matthew 12:36, Jesus is speaking, "But I say unto you, That every idle word that men shall speak, <u>they shall give account</u> thereof in the day of judgment." Because of the fact that God is omniscient, or all knowing, it is imperative for mankind to give heed to what He is telling us. Psalm 139:4, "For there is not a word in my tongue, but, lo, O lord, thou knowest it altogether." God knows our words and intent before we even speak. Go with me to the book of Hebrews, chapter 4, verse 13, the writer is speaking of God concerning this very thing, "Neither is there any creature that is not manifest in His sight: but <u>all things</u> are naked and opened unto the eyes of Him with whom we have to do." There is not a single part of our being that is hidden from God, and eventually, be it the judgment, we <u>will</u> have something to do with Him.

More instruction on how we are to control our tongue is found in Ecclesiastes 5:2, "Be not rash with thy mouth, and let not thine heart be hasty to utter anything before God: for God is in heaven, and thou upon earth: therefore let thy words be few." Don't be reckless with the words that come out of your mouth, and don't be quick to speak without thinking; have something of value to say or don't speak at all. And Proverbs 21:23 gives a clear reason for this, "Whoso keepeth his mouth and his tongue keepeth his soul from troubles." Our mouth can get us into a whole lot of trouble if we fail to use caution.

This entire exercise of learning how to control our tongue would be futile and a waste of time if it was not of such great importance to our well being as a follower of Christ. We owe Him our very best, and if not sincere, our words betray us.

Ephesians 4:29, "Let no corrupt communication proceed out of your mouth, but that which is good to the use of edifying, that it may minister grace unto the hearers." It does not take an excessive amount of intellect to understand this verse, simply follow directions!

Colossians 4:6, "Let your speech be always with grace, seasoned with salt, that ye may know how ye ought to answer every man." It is important to know "what" to answer a person when the occasion arises, "how" to answer, and to use the "salt" of Gods Word when doing so. Just to run off at the mouth and not have anything of value to share is meaningless and may end up being harmful. This is part of "tongue control." My point is found in Second Timothy 2:15, "Study to show thyself approved unto God, a workman that needeth not to be ashamed, rightly dividing the word of truth." In other words, no pun intended, we have to <u>dig in</u> and <u>study</u> the Word of God so we can <u>know</u> what we are talking about when discussing the truth of Scripture and of life and death. It is very hard to make a point if we don't know what to say or the basis of what we are talking about. We are, as Christians, instructed by Scripture to study the written Word, seek after wisdom, knowledge, and understanding, pertaining to God and how we conduct our life. The responsibility is ours if we lay claim to being a "Christian."

First Peter 3:10, "For he that will love life, and see good days, let him refrain his tongue from evil and his lips that they speak no guile." This is another very clear admonition on how and why it is wise and necessary that we are able to control the tongue.

We have gone through this rather lengthy dialogue on "words" for the purpose of being able and capable of justifying the truth of Gods Word. Because there are many in the world today that twist, subvert, deny, and simply reject Holy Scripture and label it as "myth." So the question I would ask is, are we mentally and spiritually prepared to be a defender of our faith? This has nothing to do with argument or physical confrontation.

In Second Timothy, chapter 4, verse 2, the Apostle Paul is giving his young charge some instructions that we need to follow in our Christian walk. Paul said, "Preach the <u>Word</u>; be instant in season, out of season; reprove, rebuke, exhort with <u>all longsuffering and doctrine</u>." If we are to "preach," or converse with anyone about our faith in God, we had better know <u>His Word</u>. What we say is of little consequence if not backed by Scripture.

Being "instant in season and out of season" tells me it is urgent. Be it an opportune time or a time when I must have a quick response, to be ready <u>always</u> with a good reason for my faith in God. My advice, for what it is worth, don't reprove, rebuke, or exhort anyone without the patience and ability to endure insults and possibly bodily injury for your belief. Of the utmost importance is for our "doctrine" to coincide with Biblical teaching. To simply argue with someone about Christianity is detrimental and can cause much harm. Mental and spiritual preparation, along with prudence, if we are to get the message across is essential.

I would like to use a slightly longer portion of Scripture that will more adequately sum up the thought I am attempting to convey. First Peter, chapter 3, verses 12 through 17, "For the eyes of the Lord are over the righteous and His ears are open unto their prayers: but the face of the Lord is against them that do evil." 13- "And who is he that will harm you, if ye be followers of that which is good?" 14- "But and if ye suffer for <u>righteousness sake</u>, happy are ye: and be not afraid of their terror, neither be troubled;" 15- "But <u>sanctify</u> the Lord God in your hearts: and <u>be ready always</u> to give an answer to every man that asketh you a reason of the hope that is in you with meekness and fear:" 16- "Having a good conscience; that, whereas they speak evil of you, as of evildoers, they may be ashamed that <u>falsely</u> accuse your <u>good</u> conversation in Christ." 17- "For it is better, if the will of God be so, that ye suffer for well doing, than for evil doing."

It is fact that we hear many words of condemnation and ridicule against the Bible and those who believe and practice what is taught therein. This has been the case since the inception of Christianity, and before, even until the present time. By this I mean that even before Christ, there were those who opposed God's authority and commandments. Disobedience and opposition against God's will for man on earth began in the Garden of Eden with the first human beings, Adam and Eve.

Due to the fact that enmity between God and man was perpetrated by Satan, it will continue until the time when God says enough, and the day of judgment takes place. This is the very purpose of knowing how and why we are to conduct our "mortal life" in a manner that will ensure our "immortal life."

At this point, one thing must be made perfectly clear, and that is, <u>eternity is at stake</u>! Is it possible to imagine what <u>"forever"</u> means? At some time, and no one really knows when it will happen, this physical, or mortal life that we are living, will cease to be. What happens then? Hebrews 9:27, "And as it is <u>appointed</u> unto men once to die, but after this the judgment." Also, in Romans 14, verses 11 and 12, "For it is written, as I live, saith the Lord, every knee shall bow to me, and every tongue shall confess to God." 12- "So then every one of us shall give account of himself to God."

Death is one appointment that no one will miss, and the judgment of God is our final appointment. Then what? This is the all important question because it will determine our <u>eternal destiny</u>! Because mortal life is terminal, what could possibly be more relevant and of more importance than eternity, and, where our soul will remain in existence <u>forever</u>? In only <u>one</u> of two places!

Romans 6:23, "For the wages of sin is death; but the gift of God is <u>eternal life</u> through Jesus Christ our Lord." Next, in the Gospel of John, chapter 10, verses 14, 27, and 28, Jesus tells us this, "I am the Good Shepard, and know my sheep, and am known of mine." 27- "My sheep hear my voice, and I know them, and they follow Me:" 28- "And I give unto them eternal life; and they shall never perish, neither shall any man pluck them out of my hand." Now to the book of First Peter, chapter 1, verses 4 and 5, "To an inheritance incorruptible, and undefiled, and that fadeth not away, <u>reserved in heaven</u> for you," 5- "Who are kept by the power of God through <u>faith</u> unto salvation ready to be revealed in the last time." We are also told this about the positive side of eternity, in Revelation 21:4, " And God shall wipe away all tears from their eyes; and there shall be no more death, neither sorrow, nor crying, neither shall there be any more pain: for the former things are passed away."

Now, we must view the negative side of eternity. Because this is a very unpleasant subject, we will use only a short portion of Scripture, also found in the book of Revelation, chapter 20, verses 12 through 15, "And I saw the dead, small and great, <u>stand before God</u>; and the books were opened: and another book was opened, which is the book of life: and the dead were <u>judged</u> out of those things which were written in the books, according to their works." 13- "And the sea gave up the dead which were in it; and death and hell delivered up the dead which were in them: and they were judged every man according to their works." 14- "And death and hell were cast into the lake of fire. This is the second death." 15- "And whosoever was not found written in the book of life was cast into the lake of fire." On second thought, I will also add a comment made by Jesus, found in Matthew 13, verses 41 and 42, "The Son of Man shall send forth his angels, and they shall gather out of his kingdom all things that offend, and them which do iniquity;" 42- "And shall cast them into a furnace of fire: there shall be wailing and gnashing of teeth ."

There is nothing I can add to this except to say mankind has been given the opportunity to make the choice as to where they will spend forever.

Before we continue on into the following chapters, I would like to point out two more significant words that are the essence of the entire book, and they are "Christian" and "martyr." These two words have been incorrectly and improperly used by a vast number of people when describing certain individuals or a specific act. We will begin with the dictionary meaning of "martyr."---"A person who chooses to suffer or die rather than give up his faith or his principles; a person <u>tortured</u> or <u>killed</u> because of his beliefs." Martyrdom is not to be equated or given the same meaning as "suicide," which is the act of killing oneself intentionally. A martyr is a person who suffers at the hand of someone else, and suicide is self-inflicted.

"Christian" is a word that, by many, is completely misunderstood. First, the dictionary meaning: "A person professing the belief in Jesus as the Christ, or in the religion based on the teachings of Jesus."

Let me say this, no place in the Bible can I find a prefix attached to the word "Christian." Such as, Protestant-Christian, Catholic-Christian, or any other denomination-Christian! The same holds true for any particular ethnic, or racial group of people. "Christian," is a name that stands alone and should not be joined to any specific man-created organization, culture, or race. Christianity is all-inclusive! The only legitimate claim to this title is to be a true born-again follower of Jesus Christ as defined by Scripture. Anyone can belong to, or affiliate with, an organization, but Christianity is a <u>way</u> of life!

There is a huge difference between belonging to an organization and living a certain life style designed by God.

Now we are ready to get into the substance of this book, and probably more controversy, so fasten your seat belt and let's go for a ride!

Chapter Two
A Battle With Words

I believe that we are living in a very significant time at this point of world history. There is a great deal of hateful, malicious, and accusatory rhetoric being spewed forth through our various media, radio, television, newspapers and magazines. By some very prominent and well-known persons, I might add. And also by others, who, by an act of ill-intent, or an accusation, it becomes news worthy.

The Duke University lacrosse team members who were falsely accused of rape and other crimes is a case in point. This fiasco continued for over a year before all charges were dropped. The three young men who were charged went through a great deal of anguish and finances because of the dishonesty of the prosecuting attorney. What was his motive, having no real evidence of guilt? Good question! Many hurtful words were used in this case.

What about the radio and television personality, Don Imus, who used derogatory racial and sexual remarks over the air about Rutgers University ladies basketball team? His hurtful words certainly caused a huge outcry from many, and rightfully so. However, two of his main accusers, the "Reverends?" Al Sharpton and Jesse Jackson, are men with a history of their own bigoted remarks and questionable life style.

There is so much of this loose, hateful and demeaning talk going on now days that it should be incumbent upon everyone to look in the mirror before making rash statements about others we do not agree with.

I could go on and on with comments by well-known individuals that were used to slander and hurt people they did not see eye to eye with. But I want to talk about an issue that is of great concern to me and has become a common practice by many prominent persons. This has to do with "Christian bashing," which includes "people of faith," and also "church goers" and "Bible thumpers," as Christians are referred to.

Ted Turner is a man of great entrepreneurial success, well known for his wealth and many business ventures. He refers to Christians as being "Jesus freaks," claims Christianity is for "losers," and is "intolerant," and profiles Christians as "bozos."

Rosie O'Donnell is supposed to be a comedienne. She is a lesbian, and not at all funny. Her statement is, quote, "Radical Christianity is just as threatening as radical Islam in a country like America where we have separation of church and state," end of quote. There is a long list of same-sex oriented men I could name but will mention only three of the most infamous. John Wayne Gacy, Jeffrey Dahmer, and Joseph Edward Duncan the 3rd. These individuals were serial killers and child molesters. Would Rosie like to comment on these homosexual perverts?

Linda Ronstadt is a famous country music, pop-rock singer, who had this to say, quote, "It's a real conflict for me when I go to a concert and find out somebody in the audience is a Republican or a fundamental Christian. It can cloud my enjoyment. I'd rather not know," end of quote. I don't suppose any other religious group would "cloud her enjoyment," do you?

There are many more celebrity type people who denigrate Christianity, but I won't waste anymore space with their comments. However, let me give a partial list of folks from the entertainment industry and how they died; most of them at a young age:

Hank Williams- country music singer, deceased 1953 of an accidental overdose of morphine and alcohol.

Marilyn Monroe- actress, sex symbol, deceased 1962 of barbiturate overdose, probably intentional.

Sonny Liston- heavy-weight champion boxer, deceased 1970 of a drug overdose.

Janis Joplin- rock-and-roll singer, deceased 1970 of heroin overdose.

Jimi Hendrix- rock guitarist/ singer, deceased 1970, choked on own vomit caused by sleeping -pill overdose.

John Belushi- actor and comedian, deceased 1982, overdose of cocaine and heroin.

Dennis Wilson- rock-and-roll musician with the Beach Boys band, deceased 1983 by drowning due to intoxication.

Kurt Cobain- grunge singer with the band Nirvana, deceased 1994 by gunshot after lethal dose of heroin, presumed suicide.

Cal Jammer- porn star, deceased 1995, suicide.

Tupac Shakur- rapper singer and poet, deceased 1996, gunshots from drive-by shooting.

Chris Farley- comic/ actor, deceased 1997 of an accidental overdose of cocaine and heroin.

Jam Master Jay- hip-hop singer and disk-jockey, with the band Run DMC, deceased 2002, gunshot from an unknown attacker in music studio.

Dimebag Darrell- guitarist with the band Pantera, deceased 2004, murdered.

Mitch Hedberg- comedian, deceased 2005 of drug overdose.

Anna Malle- porn actress, deceased 2006, car crash.

Anna Nicole Smith- Play Boy bunny and model, deceased 2007, prescription drug overdose.

Keep in mind that this is only a short list of people in the entertainment world who died of un-natural causes.

Some time ago I read a list of very wealthy individuals who died by committing suicide. I only bring this up as a matter that we will discuss later on. There are many others who condemn Christianity, so we will note a few of those people also.

One such person of note is the illustrious U.S. Senator from Massachusetts, Ted Kennedy. His entire life has been spent going to school, being involved in politics, and in the Congress. He claims to be a devout Catholic, but doesn't live up to his own church's beliefs; he is a proponent of abortion, and same-sex marriage. He makes outrageous accusations against his opposition political party and "right wing Christians." Kennedy has never been able to explain the death of Mary Jo Kopechne, who was left to drown in a car that the Senator drove off a bridge into the bay at Chappaquiddick Island; and not reporting it until many hours later. This event happened July 18, 1969, and still no satisfactory answer.

Senator Kennedy is only one of several Congress persons to attack Christianity by voting to pass laws contradictory to Biblical ethics. But, by the way he rants and raves, brings him front and center.

Another well known activist against true Bible Christianity is the "Reverend?" Barry W. Lynn. He is the executive director of Americans United for Separation of Church and State, and also a lawyer-lobbyist for the A.C.L.U. It has never been established that he has ever been the pastor of a church or delivered a sermon. It seems that his main role is to vilify fundamental Christian churches for exercising the right of political freedom.

Oh yes, there are many so-called "Reverends" that don't have a clue as to what Christianity is all about. What does the Bible tell us about this type of individual? Actually, there is a great amount written in Scripture about this kind of behavior, but I will only use a few references. Second Corinthians 11:13, "For such are false apostles, deceitful workers, transforming themselves into the Apostles of Christ." Next we will go to the book of Second Timothy, Chapter 3, reading verses 5, 7, and 13, "Having a form of godliness, but denying the power thereof: <u>from such turn away</u>." 7- "Ever learning, and never able to come to the knowledge of the truth." 13- "But evil men and seducers shall wax worse and worse, deceiving, and being deceived." And last, Second Peter 2: verses 1 and 2, "But there were false prophets also among the people, even as there shall be false teachers among you, who privily shall bring in damnable heresies, even denying the Lord that bought them, and bring upon themselves swift destruction." 2- "And many shall follow their pernicious ways; by reason of whom the way of truth shall be evil spoken of."

These verses are very clear an concise. There are many false teachers who are twisting the truth to fit their own ideology, even though it is contrary to Biblical teaching.

As an example I will cite part of an article from our daily newspaper, The Billings Gazette, headlined, quote, "PRO GAY ACTIVISTS TO HOLD VIGIL "A group that champions religious acceptance of lesbian, gay, and bi-sexual and transgender people was preparing to hold a vigil outside a Billings Bible college today.

Activists with the Soulforce Equality Ride were headed to Yellowstone Baptist College, 1515 S. Shiloh Road, for a peaceful demonstration set to begin at 10 A.M., according to a press release.

The faith-based group hoped to spark dialogue about the schools stance against homosexuality, said media director Brandon Kneefel.

"We know this is foreign to some places," Kneefel said. "We're here to tell them you can be gay and be Christian."

About 50 members of the organization are traveling on two buses to 32 Christian schools across the nation to "initiate discussion about faith and sexuality in communities where it is most controversial," according to the Soulforce web site." End of quote.

First of all, these people were not invited to speak at this school. Secondly, they came to create a controversy; simply because Yellowstone Bible College does not teach their brand of warped theology.

If there ever was an oxymoron statement, this was one, "We're here to tell them you can be gay and be Christian." It is <u>impossible</u> to continue in a life of sin and be a Christian at the same time! It just does not work that way, period!

Why do certain people try to <u>force</u> a confrontation on others in the guise of "Faith?" The Bible is very clear on this issue also. Beginning in Genesis 1:27 and the first half of verse 28, "So

God created man in His own image, in the image of God created He him; male and female created He them." 28- "And God blessed them, and God said unto them, Be fruitful, and multiply, and replenish the earth, and subdue it......." Also, we find in Mark 10:6 and 7, Jesus speaking, "But from the beginning of the creation God made them male and female." 7- "For this cause shall a man leave his father and mother, and cleave to his wife;" God did not instruct a man to cleave to, or adhere and cling to, or be faithful to, another man in a sexual manner. The same thing applies to women.

There is much Scripture condemning this practice. In fact, God destroyed the ancient cities of Sodom and Gomorrah for this very thing; and this is where the word "sodomy" comes from.

In human-kind, there is a strong built-in sexual drive that can be normal or deviate. Satan uses this desire to cause lust in the heart and mind of people to do wrong. Perhaps we need stronger and more clear teaching on the human anatomy!

The reason I brought up the deaths of some in the entertainment field, and how they died, was for a reason. It is the life-style that many lead and others try to emulate.

Here is an interesting statistic put out by the organization, MADD, Mothers Against Drunk Drivers: In the year 2005, there were a total of 43,443 people killed in traffic crashes, of which 16,885 were alcohol related. These are staggering figures! This information came from the National Highway Traffic Safety Administration. All in one years time! Then in 2006, the number of alcohol related deaths was 17,941; a figure released by the American Automobile Association, or Triple AAA. An increase of 1,056 deaths in one year. Compare this to the deaths of the U.S. military personnel in five plus years of war in Iraq and Afghanistan, less than 3,000. No comparison to drunk driving!

Two more short newspaper articles I will inject at this time. Number 1, quote, "N.J. GOVERNORS SUV WAS GOING 91MPH   Trenton, NJ- The sport utility vehicle carrying Gov. Jon S. Corzine was traveling about 91 mph moments before it crashed, the superintendent of state police said Tuesday.

The governor was critically injured when the vehicle crashed into a guardrail on the Garden State Parkway just north of Atlantic City last week. He apparently was not wearing his seat belt as he rode in the front passenger seat.

The speed limit along that stretch of the parkway is 65 mph.

Corzine remained in critical but stable condition Tuesday and doctors were assessing when he might be ready to breathe without a ventilator." End of quote.

It appears that if one breaks the law, and in this case two laws, speeding and seat belt, it can lead to tragedy, regardless of your status in life. The governor may not have been driving, but he had the authority to control the driver.

Second article, quote, "EDWARDS CAMPAIGN PAYS $400 FOR HAIRCUTS Washington- Looking pretty is costing John Edwards presidential campaign a lot of pennies.

The Democrat's campaign committee picked up the tab for two haircuts at $400 dollars each by celebrity stylist Joseph Torrenueva of Beverly Hills, Calif., according to a financial report filed with the Federal Election Commission.

FEC records show Edwards also availed himself of $250 in services from a trendy salon and spa in Dubuque, Iowa, and $225 in services from the Pink Sapphire in Manchester, N.H., which is described on it's web site as "a unique boutique for the mind, body and face" that caters mostly to women.

A spokeswoman for Edwards campaign did not respond to requests for comment.

Torrenueva confirmed that Edwards is a long time client and friend." End of quote.

I suppose if you are a highly paid trial lawyer, one can afford this type of cosmetic treatment. But the point is, it's vanity, pure and simple.

Let's take a look at another individual of note, and that is O. J. Simpson. His trial for murdering his wife and her male friend caused very much controversy. In my opinion, this case was a huge miscarriage of justice if there ever was one. The evidence was overwhelming as to his guilt, but because of racial accusations against one of the detectives on the case, it turned into a fiasco and he was found innocent.

In the civil trial accusing him of the wrongful death of his wife and her friend, he lost. So, how could he be guilty of one crime and not the other? The murder case was bungled from the very beginning. I guess if you are a famous black football player/ TV personality with big bucks and influence, claiming racial discrimination, you can get by with murder. Obviously!

I have absolutely no enmity or ill-feeling towards any of these folks mentioned. As was stated earlier, this was for a purpose. I could have used more examples, but these are more prominent incidents of people who made and make the news.

There are two things that all of these individuals have in common, wealth and life-style. By using the term "life-style," I am not lumping them into the same professional category, but rather in a manner that is not conducive to Christianity.

Let me state once again very emphatically, that Christianity is "a way of life," not a title that one can assume just because they say that's what they are. I understand that not all of these folks claim to be a Christian, however, many in similar circumstances do use this title.

A brief description of what constitutes being a Christian is in order at this point. It is a life that is dedicated to serving the God of the Bible, according to the terms found therein. God made the rules, not man!

A person must come to the realization that he is guilty of being a sinner, and must make restitution for his sin. Restitution is the return of what has been lost or taken away. And no, it cannot be purchased by money or good deeds. It is a <u>restoration</u> of fellowship between God and man that was destroyed because of the sin of the first man, Adam.

The Bible is quite clear as to the method for reestablishing a permanent relationship with God. After admitting a need for "forgiveness," there must be a time of "repentance." It is through Jesus, the Christ, that this repentance is made possible. It is by acceptance through "faith" in His virgin birth as Scripture proclaims, in His death on the cross at Calvary and the blood He shed, that He arose from the grave on the third day, and is presently seated at the right hand of God the Father in heaven, making intercession for those who have asked for forgiveness and believe that He has done so. From that time on we recognize that our life belongs to God and He is in control of our thoughts, our words, and our deeds; no turning back! Because, through this plan, our destination for eternity is everlasting life!

This is a completely foreign concept to those who deny Biblical doctrine. However, as was stated, we do not make up the rules, because this plan of salvation was ordained of God, the Creator of heaven and earth and all things therein, including mankind.

It is the difference between a "life-style" and "living the life" that distinguishes a true Christian from a non-believer or someone who simply lays claim to the title for a personal motive.

You might consider this a rather simplistic definition of Christianity, but God does not want it to be complicated; Satan does, and that's the reason for so much turmoil and controversy over this subject. We must also realize that Satan is in a battle against God for the souls of every person on earth. It is the age old battle of good verses evil. All that is good and righteous radiates, or emanates, from God, while all unrighteousness and evil is Satan driven.

This is the real reason for "Christian bashing" that we see so prevalent in the world today. It is because of the battle between good and evil that rages in the hearts and minds of people that causes the need for a clear understanding of Christianity.

If there is any doubt in your mind that "Christian bashing" is not for real, check it out on the internet, opinion articles in newspapers, magazines, and radio and television talk shows. Our current political presidential primary campaigns are replete with innuendo about a candidates religious beliefs. They all want to be perceived as having a certain amount of "Christian" ideology. But you can be sure that he, or she, will be maliciously assaulted verbally with character assination if they are considered to be far out "right wing" bigots. In other words, one must conform to their ideology, not what the Bible teaches. However, they all want the support of conservatives and Christian groups even if it entails being hypocritical in order to gain votes. Politics as usual, you say? This may be true, but the question arises, what type of people run for elected office? Good question! By the number of lies, scandals, crimes, and corruption commited by elected government officials, of all levels, not to mention the lowest opinion rating ever of our congress, one has to ask what has happened to integrity in this country?

I, for one, am tired of career politicians and family dynasties being entrenched in government simply to satisfy their lust for power and fame. And it appears that the general public has no recourse. The old saying that "power corrupts" is no joke, and is very obvious by the behavior of many public officials, both elected and appointed. Why is that? Because this nation, in a large measure, has become morally bankrupt.

It is very easy for one to become critical and cynical but I try hard not to do that. However, there are times when it becomes essential to point out government involvment that goes beyond the realm of decency .

For instance, the National Endowment for the Arts gave between $100,000 and $249,000 to help underwrite the Sundance Film Festival, and the PBS, the Public Broadcasting System gave between $50,000 and $99,999. Both NEA and PBS are funded primarily by our tax dollars. I will mention only two of the films shown at this "festival."

"Hounddog." starring Dakota Fanning. It is mainly about how a 12 year old girl who was raped and then struggles to come to terms with this terrible event. Most of the comments from viewers found it to be distasteful and repugnant.

"Zoo" is the other one and I don't know who starred in this film. Anyway, it is about the life of a man from Seattle who died as a result of an "unusual" encounter with a horse. In other words, a sexual encounter. Some way to spend <u>our</u> government tax money, right?

And what about government support of abortion clinics? Thousands upon thousands of babies are put to death each year with taxpayer funding!

Citizens tax money is being spent without their consent in ways that are unjust, unnecessary, contrary to the public welfare, and above all, against the commandments of Almighty God.

This "battle of words" we are enduring is going beyond mere talk and dissent into a more hostile confrontation between Christian and non-Christian. As a matter of servival, some Christians are standing up and rebutting the slander hurled at them. Not with meanness or rancor, but by kindness and love from the Word of God. Of course this has no meaning for those who disblieve that the Bible is real truth and justice.

As an older person, I cannot remember a time in American history when Christians experienced being hated for following Jesus Christ, as they are today. It has not yet reached the crisis as in other nations, but the trend of hatred toward Christianity is growing rapidly.

The news media and our "entertainment" industry ridicule and make light of anyone who stands up for Jesus Christ in public. They lead a propaganda war of stereotyping Christians into a subculture of uneducated illiterates that should have no voice in public affairs. Evan though most Americans claim a belief in God and regularly attend religious services, rarely are posetive Christian and conservative news events broadcast on the public airwaves. Network coverage of abortion and homosexuality are never done from the religious point of view. This information comes from the Washington D.C. Media research Center.

In the work place there are many documented cases of people being fired or reprimanded for making public their Christian belief. And this is becoming all too common in the occupational environment.

In the public forum, the trend is to do away with anything that has a religious, or more specifically, a Christian connotation. Taken from the Agape Press are the following: In March of 1998, the ACLU put pressure on the small town of Republic, Missouri, to remove a fish symbol from it's official logo, calling it a "secret sign of Christianity."

In April of 1998, the Rev. Patrick Mahoney was arrested for praying on the steps of the Supreme Court building. Tourists visiting Washington D.C. in 1997, were ordered by the police to stop praying in the rotunda of th U.S. Capitol. In 2003, the National Park Service removed 30 year old plaques inscribed with Bible verses at Grand Canyon National Park following complaints from the American Civil Liberties Union, or ACLU.

This is only a bare sample of incidents of this nature concerning areas that are supposed to be "public property." However, a multitude of "Gay Pride" events and other immoral acts are commited on public property with no outcry, and seemingly, tacit approval of those in authority.

The federal government infringes on the free exercise of religion in America by regulating certain churches and other religious organizations through it's tax laws. If a church was to back a specific candidate for public office they will have their tax exempt status taken away.

Possibly the most ominous and devient battlefield in the war on Christianity takes place in our public schools. The Bible and nondenominational prayer are not permitted. The Ten Commandments and other Christian displays are banned. Anything that has to do with the God of the Bible and Jesus Christ is considered bigotry and intolerant of anyone else's belief. At the same time, students are forced to hear that homosexuality is an accepted alternitive life style. And that evolution is fact rather than a theory. Some of the reading assignments in literature are plain old smut. Just don't bring up the subject of Jesus Christ and His plan of redemption, or anything of a religious nature, or Christian values, because you might hurt the feelings of some athiest or other non-believer. Your beliefs don't matter!

Now the question arises, why is there so much violence and killing taking place in our schools? Well, take away all that is good, righteous, and moral, then the alternitive, or bad side of human nature takes over. This is as sure as night follows day!

Perhaps the most devious and subtle areas in the war on Christianity is taking place in our over-esteemed judicial system. Lawyers making law means that <u>everything</u> must be litigated.

Seemingly, no end of lawsuits, frivolous or otherwise.

Judges interpreting law to suit themselves rather than following the Constitution. Violent offenders given light sentences or probation and turned loose on society to continue their criminal activity. I could cite case after case where this has happened. And even worse than that, when judges have ruled immorality as being legal and Gods Commandments as illegle.

Here is some food for thought for you to ponder over. This war of words that is going on to stiffle Christianity will continue and grow worse because the majority of the people do not have the will or the fortitude to fight on. Values based on Scripture are becoming more and more meaningless to the masses.

Chapter Three

The Fight Goes On

Do you get weary and disheartened because there seems to be no solution to the problems dividing this nation? If only we could elect the right people to public office, things will get better. If only we could somehow stop all the wars and fighting going on in the world, that surely would make things better. If only we had a national health care system in America that was given to everyone free, this would lessen the burden and we would all feel better. If only costs were low and wages high, this would solve most of our problems.

I hate to burst your bubble, but my being facetious won't solve any problems either, likewise with the afore mentioned scenarios.

The fight against Christianity is an on- going battle and it will not end until Jesus Christ returns. If reading this makes you unhappy, perhaps you should spend more time reading the Bible. The truth hurts some times but that's just the way life is. We can either conform to it, God's Word that is, or suffer the consequences for not doing so.

Forgive me if I seem rather blunt while writing this book, but it is time for God's people to face some hard, cold facts. We must take a stand against the evil that is permeating this country or we will capitulate and compromise to our own downfall.

Now, let me be absolutely clear on one thing, I am not advocating violent conflict with the adversaries of Christianity. On the contrary; our attitude must always be meek and humble, emulating the Spirit of Christ. Let me also be very explicit by stating that Christians should not just roll over and play dead when we are attacked. We have a voice that can and should be heard. I do not suggest shouting anyone down or rabble-rousing simply to gain attention. What we say and do must conform to the teachings of Holy Scripture and not just anything we come up with on the spur of the moment. In other words, we must be <u>grounded</u> in the reality of the truth of the Bible being the infallible Word of God. Simply put, if this spiritual foundation is lacking we will lose the battle.

As the title of this chapter declares, this is an ongoing conflict. We are given warning of this in the book of First Peter, chapter 5, verse 8, "Be sober, be vigilant; because your adversary the devil, as a roaring lion, walketh about, seeking whom he may devour:"

Now for a reality check. If you doubt or disbelieve that there is an actual Satan out in the world doing harm, please explain to me why all the hatred, violence and evil transpires in every corner of the globe? And, on a continual basis, not simply isolated incidents. Satan is wageing an aggressive onslaught against all that is pure and righteous; and his warfare may be violent , or subtle. Any method he can devise to deceive the hearts and minds of uncaring or unbelieving individuals will be used. There is far too much evidence for anyone to refute or disprove this statement.

Why are Christians embarrassed, insulted, shouted down, and made to look like idiots and morons and out of step with the rest of the world? It's because we <u>are</u>, and <u>should be</u>, out of step with the things of the world that are immoral, un-Godly, and just plain old sinful. This Christian bigotry is for the sole purpose of intimidating us into silence. If we are denied the right or simply choose to not speak up, how can we be the ambassadors for Christ as the Bible instructs us to be? If we believe the Gospel message, are we not to be witnesses to that fact? And it is this choice that will separate the sheep from the goats, the true believer from the phony. Some folks may consider this as being harsh, but we must keep in mind that eternity is forever!

Now, let's get into some of the things Christians are being accused of. The worldly people say that Christians are judgmental, and criticise their ways and say they are not good enough. The worldly claim that Christians are arrogant and better than them because we think we know the <u>only</u> way unto eternal life, assuming there is such a thing. Christians are accused of being ignorant. We really don't know what we are talking about because we disbelieve all other world religions.

We are supposedly uneducated. Along with being ignorant, Christians are narrow-minded, according to our critics, because we refuse to accept the so-called "science" of evolution, man-caused global warming, that a fetus is not a human being, and a host of other un-Godly worldly nonsense.

Oh yes, we want to remember that Christians are labeled as being "old fashioned," and cling to myths of bygone days. Speaking as one who has grown older, God and the Bible become more relevant as each day slips by. Christians are also categorized by a list of names that the world finds aapropriate. We are called "the extreme right wing," the "radical far right," and " Christian right," to name only a few titles that are printable.

I ask this question, how often do you see or hear criticism of the "radical left," the abortionists, the homosexual activists, and the radical environmentalists who oppose all development, etc.?

The world accuses Christians of being "sexist" and "homophobic" for not buying into the lie that people are born into an "alternitive life-style." Christians simply do not accept theory and philosophy that is contrary to Biblical theology, period!

We are now living in a very secular society that would disengage anyone from a sacred or religious belief that confirms Christianity as being valid. This worldly view and teaching are the big guns Satan is using in his attempt to defeat Biblical truth. He is making a great effort, by all means possible, to marginalize and demoralize those of us with traditional values. And underlying the entire effort is the spiritual nature of this battle for the souls of mankind.

It is very easy to observe the obvious attacks on Christianity, such as have been mentioned. However, in this country it has not reached the point of actual violence as it has in many other nations of the world. For instance, in all Muslim, Communist, and Socialist states it is illegal to be a Christian or to even be recognized as a legitimate belief. In most of these countries the penalty for doing so is death. If you find this hard to believe, it is easy to check out simply by using the internet to access the laws of any nation. Or go to your local library and search the laws and customs of a particular country. Better yet, contact any Protestant Missionary Society to learn how they are treated in countries around the world. As I have said, we in the United States haven't reached the point of out and out physical confrontation yet, but we are headed in that direction at a rapid pace.

Now, let's talk about the less obvious, or more subtle, battle that is going on against Christianity. I venture to say that our entire public educational system unions are fighting tooth and nail against anything that has to do with Biblical teaching. My, this statement will surely arouse the ire of some folks; but let the chips fall where they may. The facts are indisputable! Check out the curreculum of our learning institutions from grade shool, high school, colleges, and universities. You will find out that much of this material is of an anti-God and worldly philosophy, much of it based on theory rather than proven fact. Yes, it is put out as fact, but with no proven reliable evidence. Is this not subtle and ingenious on the part of Satan? Infiltrate the gullible and innocent minds of our young people with this insidious method of turning lies into so called "fact."

Allow me to quote Second Timothy 4:3 and 4, "For the time will come when they will not endure sound doctrine; but after their own lusts shall they heap to themselves teachers, having itching ears;" 4- "And they shall turn away their ears from the truth, and shall be turned unto fables."

The lies of evolution, that a fetus is not a human being, that there is no God of the Bible, that there is no heaven or hell as actual places, and many other lies that discredit the doctrine of Holy Scripture, are taught in the public school system; and even to a larger degree in the institutions of higher education.

Who is the perpetrator responsible for this great deception? Revelation 12: 7 through 9, "And there was war in heaven: Michael and his angels fought against the dragon; and the dragon fought and his angels," 8- "And prevailed not; neither was their place found any more in heaven." 9- "And the great dragon was cast out, that old serpent, called the Devil, and Satan, which deceiveth the whole world: he was cast out into the earth, and his angels were cast out with him."

Possibly Satans first act of deception here on earth was when he deceived Eve in the Garden of Eden. Genesis 3: 1 through 6, "Now the serpent was more subtle than any beast of the field which the Lord God had made. And he said unto the woman, Yea, hath God said, ye shall not eat of every tree of the garden?" 2- "And the woman said unto the serpent, We may eat of the fruit of the trees of the garden:" 3- "But of the fruit of the tree which is in the midst of the garden, God hath said, ye shall not eat of it, neither shall ye touch it, lest ye die." 4- "And the serpent said unto the woman, ye shall not surely die:" 5- "For God doth know that in the day ye eat thereof, then your eyes shall be opened, and ye shall be as gods, knowing good and evil." 6- "And when the woman saw that the tree was good for food, and that it was pleasant to the eyes, and a tree to be desired to make one wise, she took of the fruit thereof, and did eat, and gave also unto her husband with her; and he did eat."

I know that this is an old familiar story from the Bible, but one we must consider since it is the beginning of our sorrows as decendants of Adam and Eve.

There is also quite an array of issues involved in this short passage of Scripture. The first one being temptation. Next is guile, when Satan told Eve that God didn't really mean what He said. Thirdly, he told Eve that she wouldn't die, how horrible that would be, he implied. Number four was that she would become wise and have the knowledge to discern good and evil. Number five was the lust of the flesh because the fruit would provide food for the body. Number six was the lust of the eye because the tree was pleasant to look at.The seventh area Eve entered into was disobedience. And the eighth issue, brought on by this act of disobedience was <u>death</u> unto all mankind. Yes, this was the beginning of the entire spectrum of all sin and evil, be it pride, envy, murder, or whatever is contrary to Biblical instruction on how to live our life.

The Apostle Paul, writing to the church at Corinth, penned these words found in Second Corinthians 11:3, "But I fear, lest by any means, as the serpent beguiled Eve through his subtlety, so your minds should be corrupted from the simplicity that is in Christ."

In other words, don't believe everything you hear and read simply because it comes from "well educated experts" of some sort. There is nothing complicated or hidden in the Gospel message of salvation through Jesus, the Christ, the Son of God.

Another area of concern I would like to mention is called "prosperity theology." In my opinion, and some folks may disagree, this mind -set has caused the downfall of many who started trying to live the Christian life but gave up because things did not work out as they were led to believe. They were given the false hope that once they accepted Christ as their saviour, and had a strong enough faith to believe it, that God would also provide material blessings in the form of wealth, and success in great abundance. It would be proportional to one's faith.

This is absolutely <u>not</u> sound Biblical doctrine! I am not saying that wealth in itself is wrong; that would also be incorrect. Wealth, if gained and used properly ia truly a blessing, and we certainly need enough to take care of our needs and to share with others by various means. As far as I can determine, there are two kinds of wealth, material and spiritual. We can attain spiritual wealth in the midst of material poverty! However, "if " we obey God with our giving, according to Biblical instruction, He <u>will</u> supply all of our <u>needs</u>, and also give us extra to share with others. This I believe! The idea that becoming a Christian is a means to riches is preposterous. Such an idea is not only un-Scriptural, it defies common sense. This is simply another tool Satan uses to deceive and mislead gullible people. Yes, I do understand that there are well-to-do Christians, but most achieved success through hard work and good honest business practices; living by God's rules! Certainly, the majority of rich people are unbelievers, and to try and explain this phenanon would require a lengthy discourse, so we won't go there.

There is no "free lunch," and as long as people expect something for nothing, Christian or non-Christian, they are in for a rude awakening, Wealth can be used for either good or evil, and the Bible contains much information on this subject. Especially for those who expect government to supply all of their needs. Consider what the Apostle Paul wrote in Second Thessalonians, chapter 3, verse 10, a very much over-looked verse of Scripture, I might add, "For even when we were with you, this we <u>commanded</u> you, that if any would not work, neither should he eat." Wow! Is this harsh measures, or fairness? You decide.God is in control of <u>everything</u>, so where should we place our trust?

Many Christians have become entangled in schemes to become rich, so allow me to insert two portions of Scripture that are apporpriate to this subject. The first is Matthew 19: 23 and 24,

"Then said Jesus unto His deciples, Verily I say unto you, that a rich man shall hardly enter into the kingdom of heaven:" 24- "And again I say unto you, it is easier for a camel to go through the eye of a needle, than for a rich man to enter into the kingdom of God."

Next, we will go back to the sixth chapter in this same book, verses 19 through 21, Jesus speaking, "Lay not up for yourselves treasure upon earth, where moth and rust doth corrupt, and where thieves break through and steal:" 20- "But lay up for yourselves treasures in heaven, where neither moth nor rust doth corrupt, and where theives do not break through nor steal:" 21- "For where your treasure is, there will your heart be also."

The <u>real</u> treasure and riches we are promised of God are not material, but Spiritual.

All of that being said, there are many blessings we receive from God on a daily basis if we have our eyes open to them. Yes, even in times of adversity. In the 74 plus years that I have lived, His blessings are too numerous to count. The problem is that many Christians are not looking hard enough beyond this present life, to where our real treasure awaits us. We are, all too often, caught up in the cares of life, making our values become distorted and we want to compromise with the world.

Sorry folks, but this does not work! Compromise to a Christian can be fatal to ones spiritual man. Values set by God cannot be rescinded, amended, or changed, just to suit our own fancy. Hebrews 13:8, "Jesus Christ the <u>same</u> yesterday, and today, and forever." This applies to His teaching, His plan of salvation, and His commandments.

It is incumbent upon us as Christians to keep our thinking in perspective concerning Holy Writ. In other words, try and stay focused on what Scripture teaches. The Gospel of John, chapter 1, verse 1, "In the beginning was the Word, and the Word was with God, and the Word was God." Also, in verse 14, we find this, "And the Word was made flesh, and dwelt among us, (and we beheld His glory, the glory as the only begotten of the Father,) full of grace and truth."

This has to do with Christ Jesus coming as a man, to suffer persecution and death, to bring salvation to mankind. Listen to what He tells us in Matthew 24:35, "Heaven and earth shall pass away, but my words shall <u>not</u> pass away."

In spite of the continual and increasing battle against Christianity, God does not and will not change His plan of salvation. The world view constantly tries to change the meaning and truth of Scripture simply to accomplish the demise of accountability. In the evolutionary and secular agenda is the idea that there is no real God,as such, so no reason exists to be responsible to some far-out deity. If this was not the case, why is there such a hateful challenge to anything that represents the truth of Scripture?

Our present culture is a prime example of the battle going on for the attention and minds of our young people.The entertainment industry, be it sports, music, movies, or television, and oh yes, let's not forget the internet, are replete with immorality. And this is what we put up with on a daily basis. Newspapers, telivision, radio, and the world wide web, give us the latest scandals and stories of debauchery commited by the "stars" and well-known figures that make the news.

The sad thing is that many of our youth, and older folks alike, try very hard to emulate these obnoxious and obscene purveyors of filth. This is a tough fight simply because of their vast numbers and the publicity they receive. Especially the young people of today have an uphill battle to fight against this onslaught of smut they are faced with.

To top it off, much of the "stuff" they are taught in school is absolutely anti-Bible. It is not surprising to hear and read of shootings, sex scandals, disobedience, and the like in our schools and colleges in this day and age.

If anyone tries to bring in the Ten Commandments or anything of Christian values, brother, the fight is on! Probably the first on the scene will be the ACLU threatening a law-suit. Most institutions capitulate and cave in to the "demands" of the radical left-wing zealots. Next will come the atheists and other like-minded organizations to join the battle. We face many adversaries in the battle against righteousness. Following all of this will be our government agencies and school unions that manipulate and control curriculum that is mandated by anti-God thinkers, or so-called "experts" on education. Simply do away with anything of a "religious"conotation and the consequences are exactly what we are seeing today in our places of "education." What the Christian must understand is that this is a rageing battle and will not subside anytime soon. The minds of young people is a fertile ground for Satan to sow lies, unbelief and evil ideas. Once we are taught the lie of our creation, and a disbelief in God, the door is wide open for bad ideas to enter our thinking and lead to the culmination of wicked deeds. Read and listen to the daily news if you doubt that this is true.

I am not writing this because all of a sudden I got the wild-hare idea from out of the blue that the world is going to hell in a hand basket. On the contrary. Over many years of watching and listening, the evidence is abundant of a great moral change in this nation and around the world. Of course, much of this change has been slow and subtle because it has taken time to change the attitude and the will of the people. The older generation are dying off and the legacy of morality has become diluted and rejected by many as being "old fashioned," prudish and irrelevant. The idea today is to say, "don't tell me what to do or how to live, I have my own ideas," and " the Bible is just an old story- book of fables and thou shall not do this or that." Sad to say, but most have not been taught or read anything from this great Book of Life.

The fight continues as persecution of Christians grows stronger in the United States. Take the case of The Boy Scouts of America, of how the ACLU and radical homosexuals are trying to change the founding principles of this organization. These un-Godly tools of Satan are trying to force the Scouts to reject their commitment to God and allow homosexuals to become Scout leaders. Stop the Boy Scouts from meeting in schools and camping in "public" parks, and how the United Way and employee-giving campaigns are excluding the Scouts from receiving donations. This information is from the book, "On My Honor," written by Texas Governor, Rick Perry.

It doesn't take a rocket scientist to see what is happening in our institutions of learning, from grade school through the university system, they are trying to marginalize and eliminate religious expression connected to Christianity. Christian family values are ridiculed and mocked as being "unenlightened."

The left-wing secularists claim that people of faith in God are intolerant toward the homosexual life-style, people of other religions, and anyone who disagrees with them. This is a blatant lie! They use this "tolerance" theme to silence, repress, intimidate, and even punish those who declare the Judeo-Christian tradition that this nation was founded upon.

These world-view secularists are pushing so-called "hate crime" laws that would punish people who would disagree with them. Christians would not have the freedom of speech to express their views on very serious matters. It would become unlawful to express the Biblical teaching of human sexuality. It would disallow Christians to back a political candidate for office if they spoke of his or her opponents moral beliefs.

One would have to be blind not to see the hostility directed toward those who declare and live an explicit Judeo-Christian point of view. And I am not talking of a mere disagreement, but outright hatred. .I could cite case after case of Christian pastors and individuals who have been taken to court, prosecuted, fined, and denied the right to speak their personal beliefs because of these so-called "hate crime" laws. Yes, in the United States of America! World wide, it is even worse.

Christians who value the freedom of speech cannot ignore, or remain silent, about these heinous attacks on our liberty.

Another very crucial battle being waged against Christianity is in our judicial confirmation process. The "religious right" is the big culprit in these proceedings. If one's views are not in line with the secular fanatics they are not fit to be a judge on any Federal bench; or so they claim. It is sickening and disheartening how some of our elected law-makers hold those with Christian beliefs in disdain. They disregard completely the moral founding of this nation. And they are unwavering in their stance against Christianity, making this a tough fight..

Recognizing the fact that we will face persecution and stronger resistance as time goes on, it is essential for Christians to be prepared. Our instructions from the Word of God are found in Ephesians, chapter 6, verses 11 through 18, "Put on the whole armour of God, that ye may be able to stand against the wiles of the devil." 12- "For we wrestle not against flesh and blood, but against principalities, against powers, against the rulers of the darkness of this world, against spiritual wickedness in high places." 13- "Wherefore take unto you the whole armour of God, that ye may be able to withstand in the evil day, and having done all, to stand." 14- "Stand therefore, having your loins girt about with truth, and having on the breastplate of righteousness;" 15- "And your feet shod with the preparation of the gospel of peace;" 16- "Above all, taking the shield of faith, wherewith ye shall be able to quench all the fiery darts of the wicked." 17- "And take the helmet of salvation, and the sword of the Spirit, which is the Word of God:" 18- "Praying always with all prayer and suplication in the Spirit, and watching thereunto with all perseverance and all supplication for all saints;"

After we have put on the armour of truth, righteousness, peace, faith, and salvation, our weapon against evil must <u>always</u> be the Sword of the Spirit which is the Word of God. This armour must be accompanied with prayer for our own guidance, watching for the attack from the enemy, be persistent, and also pray for our fellow believers in Christ.

And may we <u>never</u> forget this: "For the Word of God is quick, and powerful, and sharper than any two-edged sword, piercing even to the dividing asunder of soul and spirit, and of the joints and marrow, and is a discerner of the thoughts and intents of the heart."- " Neither is there any creature that is not manifest in His sight: but all things are naked and opened unto the eyes of Him with whom we have to do." Hebrews 4: verses 12 and 13.

Wow! Let this soak in for awhile!

Chapter Four
What Is A Martyr?

At this time in history we are hearing a great deal about martyrdom. Especially coming from the turbulent Middle East countries.

The terrible disasters of September 11, 2001, was and act of martyrdom according to the adherents of Islam. Their atrocious acts of suicide bombing is also meant to fall into this category. Supposedly, they will receive great rewards in "paradise" for the killing of infidels, as instructed in their holy book, the Koran.

According to the dictionary, a martyr is a person who chooses to suffer or die rather than give up his faith or his principles; a person tortured or killed because of his beliefs. Suicide, on the other hand, is the act of killing oneself intentionally. There is a huge difference between the two acts of dying. Martyrdom is <u>forced</u> upon another, and suicide is a personal act of self-will.

In the Bible we find that the man, Stephen, was the first real martyr. He was one of seven men appointed to look after the daily distribution to the poor in the early church, or followers of Jesus Christ. Stephen's ministry was not limited to only providing for the poor. Acts 6:8 tells us, "And Stephen, full of faith and power, did great wonders and miracles among the people." Of course this drew the rath of the Jewish religious leaders of that day. Consequently, he was falsely accused of speaking blasphemous words against Moses, and against God. Because of his unflinching faith in Jesus as being the Son of God, Stephen was cast out of the city and stoned to death. Please read the account of his death., in the seventh chapter of the book of Acts in the New Testament; it is an amazing story.

While we are on this subject, let us check out some of the other true martyrs who were killed because of their faith in Jesus Christ:

John The Babtist- the immediate forerunner of Jesus, sent by God to prepare the way for the coming of the Messiah. Beheaded by King Herrod for his stance on righteousness.

The Apostle Peter- probably the most prominent of the 12 Apostles in the Gospels, and an outstanding leader in the early days of the Christian Church. The New Testament is not entirely clear about his death, but in the Gospel of John, chapter 21, verses 18 and 19, prophecys of his martyrdom. Tradition asserts that Peter went to Rome, that he labored there, and in his old age suffered martyrdom under Nero, the 5th Roman Emperor.

Andrew- the brother of Simon Peter. According to trdition, he preached the Gospel in Scyhia and was martyred in Achaia, being crucified on an X shaped cross, now called a St Andrews Cross.

James- son of Zebadee, and the elder brother of the Apostle John. He was one of Jesus' earliest disciples and one of the Apostles. He was the first martyr among the Apostles, being put to death by King Herod Agrippa, about the year A.D. 44.

James- thought to be the brother of Jesus. He is usually regarded as the author of the Epistle of James. It is said that he was martyred by the Jewish High Priest.

Paul- the Apostle, whose Hebrew name was Saul. Born of purest Jewish blood, the son of a Pharisee. Completed his studies under the famous teacher, Gamaliel. He was an acknowledged leader in Judaism, an avowed persecutor of Christianity before his conversion by Jesus on the road to Damascus. He led a remarkable life of dedication spreading the Gospel message. He was executed at Rome by being beheaded.

John- one of the first deciples of Jesus. He was the author of the Gospel of John, the three Epistles of John, and the book of Revelation. John was exiled to the island of Patmos, off the coast of Asia Minor, in the Aegean Sea, by Roman Emperor, Domition. This tiny wind swept island was one of many isolated places where the Romans banished their exiles. It is believed that John is the only Deciple of Christ who was not martyred, but died of old age in exile on this lonely island.

Judas- and I put him on the list because he played a vital role in the death of Jesus on the cross. He was one of the original 12 deciples of Christ, but died in an altogether different manner.

After the betrayal of Jesus, his remorse was so great that he commited suicide.

Of course, most people have heard the story of Jesus himself, being crucified on the cross at Calvary. Only in this case, as attested by many witnesses, He arose from the tomb on the third day of His burial. A number of days after His resurrection, also witnessed by many people, Jesus' ascension back up into Heaven occurred publicly and visibly.

I cite these few examples of the lives of true followers of Christ for a purpose. And it is beyond my ability to give a full account of all the suffering, humiliation, and punishment that the disciples of Jesus had to endure during their life time. The purpose is to relate the commitment that was willingly given for the cause of the Gospel of Christ. Men and women dedicated their very lives to tell others the way of salvation. And this is the nature of a true Christian!

These martyrs of the Bible were not radicals trying to force their belief on others by intimidation, torture, and murder. Certainly not! They brought a clear message of hope to the people, for eternity.

The subject of martyrdom was brought up because it has not gone away; in fact, it is happening today and intensifying. I refer specifically of Christians being martyred. And remember, killing ones self in order to murder others is <u>not</u> martyrdom!

In the latest information I have been able to obtain, there are 34 countries around the world that have highly restricted government policies, or practice, preventing Christians from obtaining Bibles and other Christian literature. They also have anti-Christian laws that cause Christians to be harassed, imprisoned, put to death, possessions being confiscated, and the deniel of any rights and liberties, because of their witness for Christ. These include one nation in the Western hemisphere, which is Cuba. Nine African countries. The Comoros Islands off the south east coast of Africa. Belarus, in eastern Europe. Nine countries in the Middle East. And thirteen countries in Asia. There are seventeen countries that are very hostile towards Christians, even though their governments make a feeble attempt to provide protection. All of this animosity is directed against Christians because of their non-violent pursuit of living one's faith in Jesus Christ. These countries include: Chiapas State, in Mexico; Two countries in Africa; four in the Middle East; Gaza Strip and the West Bank, in Palistine; seven countries in Asia; and Mindanao State in the Philippines.

This is a total of fiftyone countries around the world where Christians are brutally treated, and yes, even martyred. But this is not the whole story. All Islamic and communist controlled nations are violently opposed to Christianity and the nation of Israel. All socialistic dominated nations are becoming increasingly more repressive towards Christianity. Also, some South American and European countries show little tolerance.

The individual accounts of persecution are numerically impossible to mention, but here are a few incidents taken from our local newspaper just to give you an idea of what Christians have to face: Dated, 4/19/07- Istanbul, Turkey, quote, "Assailants on Wednesday slit the throats of three employees of a publishing house that distributes Bibles, the latest in a series of attacks targeting Turkey's small Christian minority.

The three victims- a German and two Turks- were found with their hands and legs bound and their throats slit at the Zirue publishing house in the central city of Malatya." End of quote.

Dated, 3/22/07- Jakarta, Indonesia, quote, "Three Islamic militants were found guility Wednesday of decapitating three Christian school girls in Indonesia and dumping their bloodied heads in nearby villages, judges said. The militants were sentenced to between 14 and 20 years in prison.

The alledged members of the al-Quida-linked Jemaah Islamiyah network left a hand written note close to the bodies of the teenagers, vowing more killings to avenge the deaths of Muslims in earlier sectarian violence on Sulawesi Island.

"Wanted- 100 more heads," said Judge Lilik Mulyadic, reciting the letters text." End of quote. Dated, 3/22/07- Tashkent, Uzbekistan, quote, "Usbek authorities have arrested a Pentecostal Christian pastor on charges of illegal proselytizing and running an unregistered religious organization.

The State Religious Affairs Committee for the predominately Muslim state said Tuesday that Dmitry Shestakov led an underground Charismatic Pentacostal church in the eastern city of Amdijan and was converting Muslims to Christianity.

The committee called him an imposter claiming he was not affiliated with the officially registered Full Gospel Pentecostal Church.

The Norway based religious freedoms group Forum 18 said Shestakov faced up to 20 years in jail for inciting religious hatred, insulting Islam and distributing banned literature. The group said police had raided Shestakov's church and house, seizing books and tapes with religious content.

In recent months, Uzbek authorities have closed or fined several Western-funded aid groups and churches for alleged attempts to convert Uzbeks to a "religion of a Protestant character." End of quote.

This is a very small sample of how Christians are treated and persecuted in Muslim controlled countries. The accounts of atrocities given by Christian missionary agencies are astounding. These acts of violence are gaining in number and severity, even though the very thought of that seems impossible.

Now don't think that these criminal acts are perpetrated against only Christians, because they are not. Dated, 3/22/07-Baghdad, Iraq, quote, "Police said Wednesday that children were used in a weekend car bombing in which the driver gained permission to park in a busy shopping area after he pointed out that he was leaving his children in the back seat"……. "Children in the back seat lowered suspician,(so) we let it move through, they parked the vehicle, the adults run out and detonated it with the children in the back seat," Maj. Gen. Michael Barbero told reporters in Washington. "Ths brutality and ruthless nature of this enemy hasn't changed." End of quote. Dated, 3/22/07- Mogadishu, Somalia, quote, "Masked gunmen dragged slain soldiers through the streets of Somalia's capital Wednesday, then set the bodies on fire as jeering crowds threw rocks and kicked the dead after a battle in a neighborhood loyal to Islamic insurgents." End of quote.

Again, let me remind you, this is only a few of countless stories that can be corroborated of such sadistic behavior.

Muslim fanatics will not only kill Jews and Christians, but also their own people along with anyone else if it serves their purpose.

Persecution of Christians is not an old story, nor a modern one. It is a continuation from early Bible times. In Old Testament days it was the adherents of the one true God of Abraham, Isaac, Jacob, and all of the believers that followed after them. In the New Testament, it was the followers of Jesus Christ, the only begotten Son of the true God of Scripture. And it has set the course of violence for what is happening around the world in this day and age.

I can remember as a youth my mother would read from "Foxes Book of Martyrs," of unthinkable things that were done to Christians from the period we refer to as "the dark ages," and they certainly were. Christians were routinely and ruthlessly punished, by burning on the stake, being fed to hungry lions, and other types of unspeakable cruelty. This was often done simply for the enjoyment of the Roman Emperors. Not a great deal has changed along those lines in some countries.

Only recently there was a deadly attack on a Jewish seminary in Jerusalem where eight students were killed and others wounded. One of the dead was a 26 year old man and the rest were young men between the ages of 15 and 19. They were gunned down by a 25 year old Palestinian from East Jerusalem.

Despite this deadly attack, Israel signaled a willingness to move ahead with the peace talks which are in progress with the Palestinians. I say all of this to bring out a very important fact, and that is: the Jewish people, as a nation, must come to grips with the truth that Jesus Christ is "the Messiah." At some point in history a remnant of the Jewish people will accept this as being true. However, before this takes place, in an attempt to bring about peace, as they are now doing, the nation of Israel will make a pact with the Antichrist in his attempt to rule the world. Of course this will be to the detriment of Israel as they will be betrayed by the Antichrist. This is an entire saga by itself so I will refrain from going there.

It is important for us to understand the true meaning of what it is to be a martyr and the real implications that are involved. First and foremost is that martyrdom is the price that one <u>willingly</u> accepts to preserve their faith and trust in Jesus as their personal savior, and the assurance of eternal life. Secondly, no one is forced into martyrdom by a religious edict, or desires it to happen . It is a choice that is made when one has to choose between their earthly death and denying the faith they have in Jesus Christ. One's mind is clear and sure concerning their destiny. I cannot believe that any person who is in their right mind would choose martyrdom if it were not for an inner assurance from God as to their eternal salvation. In reality this is the direction in which all individuals are going, probably not by being murdered, because eventually we will all face death in some manner. It is good to have that "peace that passeth understanding" which is promised through faith in The Son of God. A third logical reason for why a person would willingly give their life for a belief in Christ, is a strong relationship with Him. Without which no one could be motivated to lay down their life, being unafraid and ready to meet our Maker. I believe that it is only through a close walk with the Lord, and a <u>firm</u> belief in salvation, as promised in the Bible, that someone is able to do this.

I cannot help but marvel at the fact that there actually are people with such strength and courage. However, I also realize we are living in a world of extremes. People commit acts that are far from being usual or conventional. Deviating to the greatest degree from that which is considered normal.

To prove this point all one has to do is listen to and read the news as to what is happening all around the world. Heinous crimes and atrocities being commited by individuals and nations.

Unusual, or "abnormal" weather events that seem to be occurring more frequently than ever. These are regarded as "extreme" happenings, are they not?

For a person to readily and voluntarily give their life for Christ is being extreme to the max, according to worldly thinking. However, this has been going on since the time of Adam and Eve and their two sons, Cain and Abel. Most Christians are familiar with the story of how Abel's offering of a lamb unto God was accepted, while the offering of Cain, which was from the produce he had grown, was rejected. There is debate as to why Cain's offering was not acceptable unto God. But the Bible does state that Abel was a righteous man, while his brother Cain's works were evil.

It boils down to this: Who is the master of our life? Are we following God's directions, or those of Satan? If I may be so bold to say, there can be no straddling the fence! A person, on a personal basis, is either for God or he is aligned with that great deceiver, the devil. And, I might add, this is a commitment that may, and does at times, lead to martyrdom. The question may be asked, what causes a person to lay down their life for a love of and a belief in Jesus Christ? Let me remind you that Jesus first gave His life <u>willingly</u> for all of mankind. In the Gospel of John, chapter 15, verse 13, Jesus had this to say, "Greater love hath no man than this, that a man lay down his life for his friends." This is a very often quoted verse of Scripture, however, the next verse is crucial to all believers, verse 14, "Ye are my friends, if ye do <u>whatsoever</u> I command you."

Now the question must be asked, just who are the <u>true</u> friends of Jesus Christ? What did He say? - "<u>If ye do whatsoever I command you</u>." Going back to chapter 13 of this same book, verse 17, Jesus also said, "If ye know these things, <u>happy are ye if ye do them.</u>"

I want to continue on in the 15th chapter, verses 17 through 21, "These things I command you, that ye love one another." 18- "If the world hate you, ye know that it hated me before it hated you." 19- "If ye were of the world, the world would love his own; but because ye are not of the world, but I have chosen you out of the world, therefore the world hateth you." 20- "Remember the word that I said unto you, The servant is not greater than his Lord. If they have persecuted me, they will also persecute you; if they have kept my saying, they will keep yours also." 21- "But all these things will they do unto you for my name's sake, because they know not Him that sent me."

To better understand the true motives of a real martyr, this portion of Scripture has to sink into our mind and our thought process. Are we, in reality, willing to suffer for Jesus sake as He was willing to suffer for us? I ask myself this question quite frequently and wonder if I would be able to withstand the test of physical persecution like many in the world are now doing. This is a very sobering thought.

In the United States of America we have not, as of yet, reached this point, but is it coming? All indications tell me that we are headed down that road. If this proves to be the case, what then? From whom, or where, do we draw our strength to stand for what is right?

I whole-heartedly believe that the early and present day martyrs found the answer to that question. I also believe that not everyone will have to face martyrdom to attain eternal life because many faithful Christians have already died without going through great persecution.

That being said, it all boils down to each individuals personal relationship with Jesus Christ. As was mentioned in the previous chapter of this book, God is a <u>discerner</u> of the <u>thoughts</u> and <u>intents</u> of the heart. Another reference is found in First Samuel 16:7, "But the Lord said unto Samuel, Look not on his countenance, or on the height of his stature; because I have refused him: for the Lord seeth not as man seeth; for man looketh on the outward appearance, but the Lord looketh on the heart."

In other words, God knows us even better than we know ourselves. He knows and understands our true intentions, and capabilities; <u>nothing</u> is hidden from Him! You may ask, what point are you trying to make? Well, the bottom line is that <u>no one</u> can deceive God into believing they are righteous when they are not. He <u>knows</u> what it takes for someone to lay down his life for Him!

This should give us much food for thought and cause us to examine our own life and how sincere we are in <u>living</u> for God. Will we be able to stand against persecution and the bitter trials of life?

Tough question, but I firmly believe that one day we will all have to face this challenge, because the battle for the souls of men will not end until the return of Christ.

Chapter Five

How Sick Is America?

The title of this chapter certainly calls for an explanation. This will probably be the most difficult chapter to write of the entire book. Not so much the assemblage of words to form sentences and paragraphs, but to get across the meaning I would like to convey.

The meaning of the word "sick" is very broad and can aptly be applied to not only the physical condition of an individual, but also of an entire nation.

First of all, we must look at the symptoms that occur signaling a condition, or disorder, serving as an aid in diagnosis.Being tired and weak are early indications of sickness. Many in America today are tired and worn out from the daily grind of life and are looking for a "cure." Even though much of the problem is self-inflicted

This state of being can lead to a troubled mind that may cause a person, or nation, to become deeply disturbed or distressed. In many cases a diesease or sickness can be compounded by unsound and unwise decisions causing one to become impaired physically and mentally. At this point mankind tends to seek a more potent cure for their ailments; a medication that will bring instant healing and relief. So naturally they look to science and their fellow man to come up with the answer. Politicians in government can get the job done if we hand them enough money and power, right?

Of course when this does not happen we have a tendency to become very emotionally disturbed, exacerbating the problem to a higher level, causing more aggrevation and bitterness. This has everything to do with our mind and how we think. Now stay with me, because as I have stated, sickness involves many areas of concern that can lead to untold complications. However, I want to apply this to the condition of this country, so try to think along that line.

When we look at the body of the United States, there are several areas that have symptoms of acute sickness. The general populous, our government, the educational system, business, religion, and the entertainment industry, They all affect the over-all well being of this nation.

In our general population we are seeing more sadistic crimes being commited than ever before. We see on television and read in the news of absolutely morbid acts commited against our fellow man that must be the result of a diseased state of mind. Acts so gruesome and grisly that average people have difficulty trying to comprehend such demented behaviour. When we observe the conduct of a large segment of society, what do you see? Addictions of every sort, starting with prescription drugs. Since the government is making it easier for people to get legal drugs, this is becoming a real problem. Of course there is a great deal of illegal drug usage also and we know of the horrendous results this can cause.

Addictions can be of a various nature, but we more commonly think of alcohol, tobacco, illicit drugs, and sexual deviance as being the main ones. However, any habit can become addictive if we let it dominate our life, and this drives people into doing what they do. For instance, one can become a workaholic. Addicted to their work until it causes the break up, or severe tension, in family and among friends. People become obsessed with <u>things</u>, bigger and better houses and toys, music, sports, or whatever becomes the most important part of our life. I am not saying all of these are bad unless they become the controlling factor of how we live. It is the habitual act of doing something that we cannot seem to do without, and the life one leads becomes abnormal and unwholesome.

If one becomes deprived of a habit it may cause physical or mental discomfort. The basic cause of most habits and addiction is the search for pleasure or the relief of stress, pain, or simply from boredom. The expression "recreational drugs" comes to mind. Isn't that an oxymoron if there ever was one? And yes, addictions can, and do, lead to murder, rape, robbery, suicide, and any number of criminal acts. I am speaking of things that are of an escalating concern in this country and around the world. As the health of our nation is concerned, would you say that this is a great sickness?

Would it be fair to say that America has become infected with what I will call microorganisms of lust, hate, jealousy, pride, the desire for wealth, power, and personal pleasure? I use the term "microorganism" because many times these sicknesses start very small and seemingly undetectable at first. We see this by observing the downfall of many people of stature who were discovered to be leading a double life.

Racism is a disease that never goes away because it is perpetuated by those who profit from confrontation between ethnic groups. These people want a continual state of turmoil among races in order to become wealthy, attain power and influence, and revel in acclaimed popularity; self-indulgence comes to mind.

Black people against white people and vice versa. American Indians demanding more and more from state and federal governments. There is also a huge influx of Mexican, Asian, and Muslim people into this country that demand their voices and concerns to be heard. Many not willing, or wanting, to assimilate into the established culture of the great American Melting Pot. They want special treatment because of their culture and their religious beliefs, so the rest of

America <u>must</u> accept <u>their</u> conditions. Isn't that a crock of crap! Yes, I made that a statement, not a question. It is true that there have always been ethnic neighborhoods in our cities and towns since the United States became a nation. In the "old days," problems between neighbors were generally worked out in an amicable fashion.

This is no longer the case. Rabble-rousers travel across the country stirring up trouble wherever they think they can gather a crowd to listen as they rant and rave. These incidents make the news all the time. And that is the intention of those who stoke the hatred of individuals and mobs to cause violence and unrest among the people, who otherwise would live and let live.

Another diesese that has gripped the general public is debt. Now when one assumes debt, it is a legal obligation, or liability, that must be repaid. Many take on this responsibility without fully realizing what they are getting into. I am making good money, or "we" if it is a couple, so whatever one wants to buy, it is affordable. Max out all the loans we can acquire, plus our credit cards, and hey, we can make it! Another addiction, is it not? When people are forced back down to earth when reality hits, or they lose their job, or debilitating accidents or sickness occur, only creates more problems; and in many cases that's putting it mildly. It can, and does, turn into disaster for individuals and families. And, when this condition becomes wide spread it can affect the country as a whole. After which, politicians and governments become involved with new rules and laws that actually deepen the problems.

This nation is currently going through a housing crisis because there is a glut on the market, and also because borrowers are unable to repay lenders. Not only individuals, but large financial institutions. Also, the American dollar has been devalued to an alarming point. All of this has lead to a very weak and less powerful monetary situation.

The next area of concern, as to being unhealthy, is our government. This is the second most devastating problem for a nations health because governments, be it city, county, state, or federal, make laws and regulations that dictate our daily life. Perhaps I should include the public school systems also, as they seem to be a government within themselves. Oh well, you make the call on that one. More on this subject farther along. And

I will get to the most important concern later on also.

For the past several years, the number of elected and appointed public officials who have disgraced themselves appears to be an unending affliction. The latest scandal being the Governor of New York State, admittedly being implicated with a prostitution ring, spending a great deal of money for their services. To top it off, after being sworn into office as his replacement, the leutenant governor admitted to having affairs with a number of women while his wife was also having an affair. He blamed it on a "rough spot" in their marriage.

Another sad account is the fact that there are people in Congress who are guilty of commiting acts that would put the average joe in prison or jail for a long time. Yet these people are elected and reelected time after time, empowering themselves to set up their own little dynasty of influence and authority, to continue taking the nation down the tube of immorality and corruption. I could cite case after case but I believe you get the picture. Are you as fed up as I am of career politicians and family dynasties assuming the role of royalty and running this country as though the rest of us were nothing but a bunch of serfs? To these dregs of humanity, our Constitution has become meaningless and outdated. A very sick and deplorable situation, is it not?

A simple question to ask, and I can only assume the answer, why do politicians spend millions of dollars seeking a job that pays only a fraction of that amount in wages? Of course, after very little research, I find that the perks are unending.

Is corruption in government a sure sign that a nation is sick? Emphaticly, yes! And does this set the example for businesses and the average person to follow? I guess you will have to answer that question yourself.

When we drive into the gas station to fill the tank of our automobile, we are again reminded of the "energy" situation. And this has politics written all over it!

In the United States, our government, and the environmentalists, will only allow partial development of this country's natural resources. Yet, people continue to holler and scream because of the high cost of gasoline and the outrageous profits of the "big oil" companies. This not only pertains to oil but also the timber and mining industries.

I am sick and tired (no pun intended) of all the claims that development will destroy our environment and endanger all the animals, birds, fish, and bugs! It may come as a shock to the uninformed, but there are methods to develop resources that cause no damage to anything, except to those with a vested interest in stopping progress.

Now the real mystery comes when even the so-called "green energy" projects such as wind, solar, hydro power, and thermal, are also attacked and taken to litigation. The only ones profiting from this are the nut-case environmentalists who file suit, their lawyers, and the entire legal system. Which is a problem in itself; a <u>very bad</u> problem!

What about the government being unable and unwilling to secure our borders? Is this not a farce and a huge accident just waiting to happen? It is unbelievable that this problem could not have been solved years ago. Here again we have special interests, and government bickering, preventing any rational solutions. Does this sound familiar?

I have read an account that this present Congress is rated the worst in history. What we have is political correctness gone berserk! Roe vs. Wade, the McCain-Feingold Act, nutty laws concerning the environment, endangered species, and so-called "hate crime" laws, to name only a few that are detrimental to this country.

The big political push at the moment is man-caused global warming, or "climate change,"which will cause a huge financial drain on our economy. Not only in the terms of direct financing, but also the untold cost to industry in order to comply with the new punitive laws that are being considered.

This nation does not even have the ambition or simple decency to clean up the common trash that litters our streets and countryside. So how are we supposed to control God's elements? This is unmitigated stupidity, simply inviting disaster! This "global warming" fiasco has become politicized world wide, so all I can say is , may the Good Lord help us! This issue will be studied to death, argued over, and debated until nothing is resolved. Except, tons of tax money will be spent in a meaningless and phony endeavor, accomplishing nothing .

Next up on our list, as I promised, is the educational system we revere so much. This has become a sacred cow, and in my view, a religion in itself, with an insatiable appetite for more money and influence. Filled with so-called experts whose gratification comes from some new theory that they claim as fact.

Let's keep in mind that education, much of which condemns Christianity, and teaches the exact opposite, is no panacea for the ills and misfortunes of mankind. By their actions and words, many professors in our institutions of higher learning are nothing more than raving lunatics. In my humble opinion of course.

God, and most things that have a righteous connotation are either ridiculed or simply not allowed for discussion. The behavior we see in our schools and colleges are proof positive of this fact. Disrespect, shootings, sex between students and teachers, and,oh yes, the un-Godly curriculum that is taught as though it were fact. We must not forget this.The social conduct of both teachers and students has become increasingly more lewd and unprincipled. No morals and no thought as to the repercussions of bad behavior. Now, I don't want to be misunderstood. I believe education is essential, and good, as long as it <u>includes</u> that which <u>is</u> good! And when we discount the effects of Godliness and righteousness, it is no longer good for the betterment of a nation. Many may consider this as bad medicine, but on the other hand, just look at the general attitude of students who are "educated" in our public schools.

The results of secular education speak loud an clear so no more elaboration is needed; except to say that the system is very anemic, and vitally in need of a shot of morality to get back on track. It does not take a great deal of brain power to understand that this is definitely a broken situation.. I will go no further on this subject for fear that some may think I am simply a ranting nut case.

Now we will briefly go into the area of "business," of which there are basically three types. Mom and Pop, or family business, small to medium sized companies, and what is referred to as "big" business.

The one thing they all have in common is regulation, and this entails a multitude of laws and rules that govern the way they coduct business. Before I continue, let me say that not all regulation is bad; I do not want to make that implication because many times it depends on the nature of the business.

I do know from the experience of owning a quite small food manufacturing business, that some laws are very restrictive and highly questionable as to their relevance. Many of them are used simply to garner a fee for some unnecessary, bureaucratic, government appointed agency whose members know little, or nothing, of the businesses they control. It did not matter if I was showing a profit, or having a loss, the cost of fees, licesence, and reports, were to be paid on time with no exceptions, or my business would be shut down. And it is without question that the hoops larger companies must jump through are even more severe.

There is an unreasonable amount of restrictions, regulations, and pressure, applied to business to be politically correct and environmentally friendly without any consideration as to the cost, or the consequences, regarding the business or the consumer.

Also, there are laws mandating the employment of minority employees, the minimum wage act, non-discrimination as to a persons sexual preferance even if it is contrary to the employers personal religious belief and policy. This is only a short list of the most egregious laws that stipulate exactly how business is to operate. Believe me, there are many more, depending upon the size of the company.

We must not forget the Labor Unions, in conjunction with the U.S. Department of Labor, which have caused the demise of many businesses, by way of their unyielding demands forced upon the employer.

I understand that there are also businesses that take advantage of employees, stockholders, and the consuming public. And I make no excuses for them because corruption and greed is every bit as wrong in business as it is in any other area of life.

I bring these concerns to your attention simply to point out the fact that any additional cost required of business is ultimately paid for by families and individuals, adding to their problem of making ends meet. Which is another cause of depression and the feeling of futility.

Next on my list of national sickness is the "entertainment" industry. With Hollywood, and by this I am referring to the American movie industry, as being the worst, in my opinion. Followed by the "music" business coming in at a close second, with "sports" at the number three spot.

By now you are probably asking, what is wrong with your mind? Everyone enjoys movies, music and sports, which most people are into at some level. Bingo! It's not that so many people are "into" these things, but rather, what influence are they having on people?

I am trying to write this book with a wholesome Christian perspective concerning the consequences and attitude certain things bring to this nation, and people in general.

This particular segment of our society can be especially harmful because of the "role-model" figures that many try to emulate. They are in the public eye because of their fame for the things they do and accomplish. The shame is that much of this "fame," or notoriety, is the result of immoral, or some other form of bad behavior.

The questions I have been bothered with for some time are, why do these people receive so much attention from the media, and why are their opinions so sought after? Evidently, many people view them as well-springs of intelectual grandeur; when in reality, judging from their words and actions, they display nothing more than feeble mindedness associated with a moronic attitude. In close resemblance to many of our esteemed political "leaders." And this is not an eternal judgment that I am pronouncing, I will leave that decision for God to make, but simply stating a behavior pattern that is quite evident. By one's words and deeds, we can have a pretty good look at a person's true character.

A huge amount of space and time is taken up in newspapers and television concerning "movie- stars" and "stars" of all the various sports. Generally speaking, most of this information is irrelevant as to how the average person lives his or her daily life. So, what is the great facination with all of these people of such tremendous fame and fortune?

Certainly, much has to do with curiosity, but probably there is a great deal of envy involved also, don't you suppose? Most famous people are hounded by photo-journalists trying to take pictures for sale to tabloids that thrive on gossip.

I believe that many are taken up with the rich and famous because they think their own life is dull and unglamorous. This brings up another valid question, why is there so much dissatisfaction in life when, in this country at least, we have it pretty good? O.k., I will offer an opinion. Mankind is searching for "something" to give meaning to life. Most of us do not have the wealth or the means to do great and noteable deeds, so we try to imitate, or follow after those who do make the news. The problem lies in the fact that most people are pursuing things of no earthly value, and certainly, of no eternal value! In other words, the majority of the people in America have their heads in a cloud and are being mystified by reality. Living in a dream world, always wishing and striving for bigger and better things to fulfill our carnal appitite, that more often than not, leads to heartache or disaster.

We see evidence of this sickness on an increasing scale. With addictions, infidelity, and unbelievable crimes being commited on a daily basis, is there any answer for all of this? There is a reason why I bring all of these issues to your attention. Because, in some way, they all contribute to the psychological and physical well-being of every individual, and the entire nation as well. They determine the way we react to our fellow man, and cope with the struggles of life.

Now, what I have to say may be offencive to some, but I feel an obligation to do so, regardless of any criticism I might receive.

It all has to do with our "inner-man," or our "spiritual being." The part of us that God has placed within this body of flesh, which will live on, throughout eternity. Granted, not everyone believes in such a thing, but will ultimately have to face that decision in the day of judgment.

Now, let's cut to the heart of the matter. Regardless of how much of this worlds goods you might accumulate, or how famous and powerful you become, it <u>cannot</u> measure up to the value of your soul, destined to spend eternity in one of two places. I simply ask that you think deeply, and often, on where you are headed, and, are you ready?

Yes, I believe this nation is very sick.

Chapter Six
Religion- Good Or Bad?

We will now delve into that area of national sickness that I consider the most serious, and devicive. Religion has become a very hot topic and I would like to present a layman's perspective on this subject. Some folks have a strong belief in their particular faith while others can take it or leave it, rather non-committal, having no definite view one way or the other. On the other hand, there are avowed atheists and agnostics who make the claim that all religion is nonsense and a figment of one's imagination. More noticeably nowadays, there are religious fanatics who violently oppose any other belief that differs from their own particular brand of theology, and will commit horrendous acts of atrocity against "unbelievers" and "infidels."

Because I am writing this book based on a reflection of one's faith in God, we must turn to the Living Book for consultation. I would like for us to fix our mind on, and seriously contemplate, what is written in Holy Scripture.

In the book of James, chapter 1, verses 26 and 27, "If any man among you seem to be religious, and bridleth not his tongue, but deceiveth his own heart, this man's religion is vain." 27- "Pure religion and undefiled before God and the Father is this, To visit the fatherless and widows in their affliction, and to keep himself unspotted from the world."

Now this sounds like a very simplistic rendering of the meaning of "religion," does it not? When we look at the dictionary definition of this word it becomes a little more complicated. We begin with the most common meaning, quote- "1(a)- belief in a devine or superhuman power or powers to be obeyed and worshiped as the creator and ruler of the universe. (b)- expression of such a belief in conduct and ritual. 2(a)- any specific system of belief, worship, conduct, etc., often involving a code of ethics and a philosophy. (b)- any system of beliefs , practices, ethical values, etc., resembling, suggestive of, or likened to such a system (humanism as a religion). 3- the community (to enter religion). 4- any object of conscientious regard and pursuit- get religion. (1)- to become religious. (2)- to become very conscientious or earnest about something." End of quote.

Wow! A kind of repetitious and anything goes philosophy as long as one is sincere in what they believe. Any idea can become a "religion" if we want to make it one. This is <u>not</u> true Christianity!

There is much to do about visiting the fatherless and widows, as was stated in the Scripture I quoted from the book of James. And I do not belittle this duty that is placed upon us. However, there is less heed paid to the part in the 26th verse about, "and bridleth not his tongue," and the last part of the 27th verse that states, "and to keep himself unspotted from the world." This was not made clear in the dictionary meaning of the word "religion." We can have a "belief" in "anything" and call it religious, according to worldly thinking. And this is where Christianity differs from <u>all</u> other religions, or "beliefs."

Again, reading from the book of James, same chapter, verses 13 through 15, "Let no man say when he is tempted, I am tempted of God: for God cannot be tempted with evil, neither tempteth He any man:" 14- "But every man is tempted, when he is drawn away of his own lust, and enticed."15- "Then when lust hath conceived, it bringeth forth sin: and sin, when it is finished, bringeth forth death."

The basis upon which Christianity rests, is the fact that mankind must repent of sin in order to obtain eternal life, and this can only be accomplished through faith in Jesus Christ as Savior and Lord, with the Holy Bible being the infallible Word of God. This concept entails the same simplicity as the Biblical rendition of "religion," as previously quoted, and "to keep ourselves unspotted from the world." Do I believe that Christians are perfect people? Absolutely not! Because we still live in a sinful world and have the same temptations as everyone else. However, if, and that's a big if, a person honestly tries to "keep himself unspotted from the world" by obeying Gods commandments, He will give us the strength and grace to overcome all temptation if one retains a repentant heart.

As a Christian, we are required to <u>live a life</u> apart from sin and all unrighteousness. This is a stumbling block for most people because it infringes upon their lusts and desires.

I have said all of this in order to view certain individuals and how they use, and have used repeatedly, religion for personal gain. And I am not judging anyone, simply making a comparison of their life style and what is taught in the Bible. The people I will mention are merely a sample of a multitude who corrupt the meaning of a true Christian. These being the more prominent and widely publicized.

Jim and Tammy Faye Bakker, who started and operated the PTL Ministry. In 1986, Jim Bakker was sent to prison for misappropriating church funds for his own use. He was also accused of bi-sexual misconduct. Tammy Faye divorced Jim while he was in prison and married his one-time best friend. She died of cancer in 2007. Since his release from prison, Jim Bakker has gone back into the ministry. And yes, God does give people the opportunity to repent.

Jimmy Swaggart- when his troubles were first revealed, was in 1986 also. He was accused of using prostitutes on several occasions. He was put out of the church denomination that he was affiliated with. Currently, he is still in the ministry, associated with family members.

Marvin Gorman- a minister of a Pentacostal denomination, was accused of having an affair with a member of his congregation. He blamed Jimmy Swaggart for his downfall, and hired a private investegator to tail Swaggart and take pictures of him with a prostitute, which in turn caused the downfall of Jimmy Swaggart. Gorman, along with his wife, is still in the ministry.

Bishop Thomas Wesley Weeks- had a pre-marital affair with a lady preacher named Jaunita Bynum and were later married, and divorced, after Weeks severely beat her . He has remarried an is still in the ministry.

The latest minister of prominence, as of this writing, with a stellar resume I might add, to succumb to worldly lust is the Rev. Ted Haggard. Who, with his wife, founded New Life Church in Colorado Springs, Colorado, which became a mega-church. He became entangled in a homosexual scandal, and was forced to resign from his church.

Minister Louis Farrakhan- heads the Nation of Islam, a radical black seperatist organization. This group was founded in Detroit, Michigan, in the 1930's. Farrakhan was actually born Louis Eugene Walcott, somewhere in the Carrabean, on May 11, 1933. Along with his mother, he immigrated to the U.S.A. when quite young, eventually became a calypso musician and singer. While on a musical engagement to Detroit, he was introduced to the Nation of Islam and joined the organization. He has a long history of being very anti-white, anti-semitic, and basically anti-American. Even wanting to create a separate "black state" within this country. He feels that Europe and America "owes" black people "reparations" for mistreating them. The Nation of Islam does not follow a true Muslim belief. It is actually a self-proclaimed racist organization with very different views from Koranic Islam, yet similar in some ways. Farrakhan has preached his hatred of Jews and white people in other countries also, mainly in Africa.

Rev. Jesse Jackson- formed the non-profit Rainbow Push Coalition, a black activist group supposedly fighting for racial equality. Rev. Jackson has become very wealthy, and has a son in Congress, from Illinios. He has also fathered a child with one of the co-workers in his organization, while still being married to his current wife.

Rev. Al Sharpton- of New York City, another black activist preacher whose occupation is conducting protest rallies and marches against white people if he merely thinks a black person is being discriminated against. He is evidently able to garner enough support from his followers to travel all over the country with his protests. And to live a lavish life- style. He also is divorced from his wife.

Rev.Dr. Jeremiah Wright- former pastor of one of the largest black churches in Chicago, Ill. Rev. Wright is a proponent of the "Black Liberation Theology" movement. He finds inspiration in the writings of two very prominent theologians with a strange view of Christianity, to say the least. Most of their ideology is very depressing in light of Biblical teaching.

One of these two men is the Rev. Dr. James Cone, Professor of Systematic Theology at Union Theological Seminary in   New York City. Allow me to present a quote from Dr. Cone, "The turn to blackness was an even deeper conversion-experience than the turn to Jesus. Blackness opened my eyes to see African-American history and culture as one of the most insightful sources for knowing about God." End of quote. He accuses "white" Christians of trying to keep Christianity exclusive. And some of his other teaching is just as ridiculous. Implying that white people are the reason for all bad things that happen to black people.

The second mentor of Dr. Wright is the Rev. Dr. Dwight Hopkins, professor at the University of Chicago Divinity School. His bio is working as a constructive theologian in areas of Contemporary Models of Theology, Black Theology, and Liberation Theologies. Sounds impressive, but all it amounts to is simply giving his own personal views on theology as it pertains to black people. He is a friend of Louis Farrakhan; which speaks for itself.

Now, the reason I specifically mentioned these black ministers is to point out a growing trend among black churches to embrace a "social gospel," and to depart from the true Gospel of the Bible. Churches have been a very strong factor in the black community ever since the days of slavery. However, this devicive "new theology" has only harmed relations between the black and white races.

Some of the above men whom I have mentioned, succumbed to the temptations of lust, greed, and self-agrandizement, while others perpetuate hatred between races for the same reasons.

It matters not as to the color of our skin, because with God our outward appearance does not determine the destination of our soul. The deciding factor is what comes from the heart.

Yes, there are also "white" racist groups and individuals, such as the White Supremacists, the Skin Heads, and the Aryon Nation. These groups are not well organized, as most of their leaders are in prison, or have been.

God is not partial to any race and that also includes His Chosen People, the Jews, for they have suffered greatly and continue to do so. We will get deeper into this subject further along in the book.

In Romans 2:11, we learn this, "For there is no respect of persons with God." A very succinct and easily understood statement!

Colossians 3:25, "But he that doeth wrong shall receive for the wrong which he hath done: and there is no respect of persons."

Second Chronicles 19:7, "Wherefore now let the fear of the Lord be upon you; take heed and do it: for there is no iniquity with the Lord our God, nor respect of persons, nor taking of gifts."

This is a warning that we must understand. God does not condone sin of any sort, and because of this, we cannot expect special treatment. And, God <u>cannot</u> be bribed! He does not esteem one man above another because of skin color, your position in society, your wealth, your power, or for any other reason. We <u>all</u> start out on an equal playing field as far as God is concerned. I will be so bold as to say this, Christianity is the <u>only</u> faith where one will find true equality. The common thread that binds Christians together is a faith in Jesus Christ as the Savior of mankind, and salvation as outlined in His Holy Word, the Bible.

Now, we could go into any number of religious beliefs, and I have examined many, but <u>none</u> hold to this criterion: that our Heavenly Father is only accessible through His only begotten Son, Jesus, the Christ. And, how the Bible instructs mankind to accept His gift of salvation, for eternity. Yes, this is a *"forever"* gift if we are willing to accept His terms and <u>live</u> for Him.

That being said, we will examine a little deeper into the fact that Christianity is neither racist or preferential in order to become a follower of Jesus.

Leviticus 19:15, "Ye shall do no unrighteousness in judgment: thou shalt not respect the person of the poor, nor honour the person of the mighty: but in righteousness shalt thou judge thy neighbor."

Do you get this? We are <u>allowed</u> to judge a person by their character, by their words and deeds, and by the way they live. This is <u>not</u> a judgment into condemnation, because that is God's responsibility. This is a determination of "what you see is what you get." In other words, when we observe certain behavior, we know what to expect.

This goes to the very heart of how our judicial system is functioning, and also what many so-called Christian leaders are preaching. Making laws and convincing people to do that which is contrary to righteousness and Biblical instruction. They are replacing what is good, for what is evil.

Proverbs 24:23, "These things also belong to the wise. It is not good to have respect of persons in judgment." Is it wise to judge someone because of their race, or their power and wealth? Is it wise to judge someone because they are poor and without influence? Absolutely not! That's a "no-brainer."

But of course we know this happens more times than not. It is especially harmful when judgment is used to divide one segment of the population from another, creating strife and bitterness.

First Timothy 5:21, The writing of the Apostle Paul, "I charge thee before God, and the Lord Jesus Christ, and the elect angels, that thou observe these things withour preferring one before another, doing nothing by partiality."

Paul was using all Heavenly authority to instruct and advise Timothy to be accountable for treating all men fairly. We would do well to follow this instruction also.

James 3:17, "But the wisdom that is from above is first pure, then peaceable, gentle, and easy to be entreated, full of mercy and good fruits, without partiality, and without hypocrisy."

If any cult, religious belief, or anyone claiming Christianity, is lacking in any of these areas, their wisdom is not of God and they are living an illusion of deception and pretense of what is good and righteous.

Let us go into another area I refer to as "personality disorder." It will be Holy Scripture pointing out the reason we see a great apostasy of religion.

The book of Jude, in the New Testament, for all who are not familiar with the Bible. Jude is only one short chapter in length. Verse 16, "There are murmurers, complainers, walking after their own lusts; and their mouth speaketh great swelling words, having men's persons in admiration because of advantage."

To murmur usually suggests dissatisfaction and anger, and we know what it means to complain about things we are not satisfied with, Usually carried out by those with an ulterior motive of lust, greed, and self-interest. Many of these are people with the advantage of a "bully-pulpit" of some sort, seeking fame and admiration of men. Does this not sound all too familiar?

More instruction from the Apostle Paul to Timothy is found in Second Timothy 4:2 through 4, "Preach the Word, be instant in season, out of season; reprove, rebuke, exhort with all longsuffering and doctrine." 3- "For the time will come when they will not endure sound doctrine; but after their own lusts shall they heap to themselves teachers, having itching ears;" 4- "And they shall turn away their ears from the truth, and shall be turned unto fables."

Certainly, this has been the modus operandi of Satan since the time he was kicked out of Heaven. However, I do believe the Devil is working overtime in this day and age because he knows his time is short.

So-called "reverends" are telling people all kinds of half-truths and preaching a "feel good" theology with very polished and smooth sounding oratory to beguile their foolish and simple minded followers who reject the truth of Holy Scripture. Or getting them all pumped up about how unfair their lot in life is. Turning away from Godliness and promoting an anti-Christ dogma that appeals to the base nature and "feelings" of those that listen to them.

Paul admonished Timothy to preach the "Word," not some other doctrine that is conceived of men. Hold fast to what is taught in Scripture and do not deviate from it's truth. To do otherwise will deceive and lead others astray.

Romans, chapter 1, verses 20 through 25, "For the invisible things of Him from the creation of the world are clearly seen, being understood by the things that are made, even His eternal power and Godhead; so that they are without excuse:" 21- "Because that, when they knew God, they glorified Him not as God, neither were thankful; but became vain in their imaginations, and their foolish heart was darkened," 22- "Professing themselves to be wise, they became fools," 23- "And changed the glory of the uncorruptable God into an image made like to corruptible man, and to birds, and fourfooted beasts, and creeping things." 24- "Wherefore God also gave them up to uncleanness through the lusts of their own hearts, to dishonour their own bodies between themselves:" 25- "Who changed the truth of God into a lie, and worshipped and served the creature more than the Creator, who is blessed forever. Amen."

Please read the remaining seven verses of this chapter if you want the rest of the story concerning the distortion of truth. It speaks of the very day in which we live.

Second Thessalonians, chapter 2, verses 9 through 12, "Even him, whose coming is after the working of Satan with all power and signs and lying wonders," 10- "And with all deceivableness of unrighteousness in them that perish; because they received not the love of the truth, that they might be saved." 11- "And for this cause God shall send them strong delusion, that they should believe a lie." 12- "That they all might be damned who believed not the truth, but had pleasure in unrighteousness."

This is very powerful and revealing Scripture, and an apt description of many who claim to be religious leaders and preachers of the Gospel. The Bible tells us that we are without excuse when we turn our back on the truth of God's Word, and turn it into a lie for self gratification, and to lead others away from God's plan of salvation.

Scripture contains much information about those who teach and practice a false doctrine, so allow me to give you a sample with these three verses found in Second Peter, chapter 2, verses 14, 15, and 18, "Having eyes full of adultery, and that cannot cease from sin; beguiling unstable souls: an heart they have exercised with covetous practices; cursed children:" 15- "Which have forsaken the right way, and are gone astray, following the way of Balaam the son of Bosor, who loved the wages of unrighteousness;" 18- "For when they speak great swelling words of vanity, they allure through the lusts of the flesh, through much wantonness, those that were clean escaped from them who live in error."

Balaam was a diviner, someone who claims special powers. He was a prophet of Old Testament times, who once done the will of God concerning the Children of Israel, but later turned away from God to lead the people astray. Do you see a similarity here? This false teacher was destroyed by God's judgment.

I hope you understand why this is the most serious problem that true Christianity has to confront in the United States of America in our present time. Many, who should be telling the good news of the Gospel and exposing sin, in reality, are leading people down the path to eternal destruction. It is bad enough for an individual to choose the wrong way, but even worse when our leaders influence others to follow a lie, and consequently lose their soul for eternity.

Now, what does Jesus have to say about this type of false teacher, preacher, or minister? Matthew, chapter 7, verses 21 through 23, "Not every one that saith unto me, Lord, Lord, shall enter into the kingdom of heaven; but he that doeth the will of my Father which is in heaven." 22- "Many will say to me in that day, Lord, Lord, have we not prophesied in thy name? and in thy name have cast out devils? And in thy name done many wonderful works?" 23- "And then will I profess unto them, I never knew you: depart from me, ye that work iniquity."

This is a very sad story, when Christ said that there will be <u>many</u> who claim to have done His will, but in reality were living a lie. And there will be no excuse for those who commit unrighteous acts, who live in wickedness, and are unjust.

In Second Corinthians 11:13, the Apostle Paul described them this way, "For such are false apostles, deceitful workers, transforming themselves into the apostles of Christ."

And also in Romans, chapter 3, verses 13 and 18, "Their throat is an open sepulchre; with their tongues they have used deceit; the poison of asps is under their lips:" 18- "There is no fear of God before their eyes."

Second Peter 2:17, "These are wells without water, clouds that are carried with a tempest: to whom the mist of darkness is reserved for ever."

Jude, verse 13, "Raging waves of the sea, foaming out their own shame; wandering stars, to whom is reserved the blackness of darkness for ever."

For our final characterazation of false teachers, we will return to the book of Second Peter, 2:12,

"But these, as natural brute beasts, made to be taken and destroyed, speak evil of the things they understand not; and shall utterly perish in their own corruption;"

These are all very sobering portions of Scripture. They should cause everyone to stop and think about our own life and the consequences we will face in the day of judgment, for all eternity.

For what it is worth, the question has come to my mind, when, and if, we are to arrive in heaven, who will we find there? Or will we be surprised by who we do <u>not</u> see?

Knowing what the Scripture tells of those who are phony, it makes me wonder at times, because in our finite, mortal mind it may be difficult to distinguish who is proclaiming the truth and who is not.

That being said, the responsibility lies with each individual to study God's Word, ask for His wisdom, and allow the Holy Spirit to direct our thinking.

Is it possible to find the mind of God for our life? According to Scripture it is, <u>if</u> we are sincere in our desire to do so.

Deuteronomy 4:29, "But if from thence thou shalt seek the Lord thy God, thou <u>shalt</u> find Him, if thou seek Him with all thy heart and with all thy soul."

Once again I must say, Christianity is more than a "religion," it is a way of life!

Chapter Seven

Is America Now An Athiest Nation?

With all of the hype about religion now days, one could assume that this is a God fearing country. However, being religious does not automatically make us believers in God; the true God of the Bible.

It is a well known fact that America was founded on Judeo-Christian values, from which most of our laws originate. Anyway, that used to be the case but does not seem to hold true any longer when we observe the attitude towards Christianity in our present day society. I am of the opinion that our founding fathers would not recognize the country they formed two hundred plus years ago.

We are not the self-reliant people that we once were. Our dependency is on the government to take care of our every need, or so it seems. At one time this was called socialism. Just have government agencies dole out to the masses only what controlling bureaucrats deem necessary. It is amazing to me when I read the meaning of liberalism. It is the first step toward outright socialism, and definitely not how this nation was ment to function. According to the dictionary, liberalism is a movement advocating a broad interpretation of the Bible, freedom from rigid doctrine and authoritarianism.

I don't quite understand what a <u>broad</u> interpretation of the Bible is supposed to mean. Except to allow anyone to twist the meaning of what God has said, to that of what man perceives or imagines.

I do understand why people want to be free of a rigid doctrine and someone who has dictatorial power over them. And , if you want to put a spin on it, this could seemingly apply to Biblical doctrine. But that is not at all accurate. To be a beleiver and follower of Bible instruction is completely, 100%, voluntary! On the other hand, liberalism and socialism want the government agencies to have the power to force their decrees upon the people.

Another meaning of the word "liberal," is giving freely and generously. Is it not strange how this word has been changed by socialist thinkers to promote their agenda? The same as the word "gay" is being used to describe homosexuals. It is no wonder that they so easily twist the meaning of God's word to suit their own fancy.

I am reminded again of this verse of Scripture, found in Romans 1:22, "Professing themselves to be wise, they became fools."

Let's take a look at our present day culture. That is if you can stand the shock and awe of it all.

Cohabitation and homosexual marriage is a "good," (and I use this word with tongue in cheek) place to start. What happened to the strong family unit? Both of these "life-styles" are killers of that instution . And the attitude of the general public is, ho-hum, what's the big deal? Marriage and family was an ordinance set up by God to be obeyed by the people. Not something to be taken lightly or scoffed at. Broken marriages, shacking-up, and "alternitive" life- styles are not God's   way of living by any stretch of the imagination.

Eat, drink, and be merry is the dominant attitude of the majority. Oh yes, people work very hard to fulfill these three strong desires. An epidemic of obesity in our population is proof of the eating addiction. And if that isn't enough, simply observe people eating in "all you can eat" restaurants and you will get the picture.

We all know what drinking is; from soft drinks to alcoholic beverages and the bottled water craze. I add that last item for a little humor, but everywhere you go , and even on television, you can't get away from someone having a bottle of water. In some cases I have often wondered if it was only water in those bottles!

O course, it is the "strong drink" that I am talking about. There is a great health concern about the use of tobacco and much restriction and taxes placed upon this product. But what about alcoholic beverages? Yes, alcohol is definitely regulated. Simply to control the proliferation of booze to those willing to pay the price for selling the stuff. In most supermarkets the beer and wine sections are very prominent and quite large.

Liquor stores, bars, and casinos selling the "hard" stuff are doing a land office business.

I believe that those lawmakers who regulate alcohol for consumption like to have a nip of "joy-juice" more than just now and then for their own pleasure. So why make it overly restrictive? And aren't we doing a lot of good with all the taxes collected on alcohol? I would need a lot of proven examples on this last question in order to say, yes.

According to our governments own statistics, along with the American Automobile Association, more people are killed in alcohol related auto accidents in one year, compared to the deaths in five plus years of the war in Iraq! Yet, we don't hear the same level of rhetoric about this American tragedy, do we? And why not?

A good question, but not difficult to answer. War does not bring the "personal pleasure" that comes in a bottle of liquor. Is that answer straight forward enough?

Next we will tackle the realm of being "merry." This subject is all about having fun, laughter, and being festive. And this fairly well sums up the attitude of most Americans; fun and games, that's what life is all about. It seems to me that, as a people, we are constantly looking for a new and better type of entertainment, or a new toy we hope to find pleasure in.

The fact of the matter is that over eating and drinking usually causes an upset stomach, acid indigestion, a hangover, or worse. And the "things" we seek pleasure in are short lived and temporary in bringing satisfaction. This fleeting gratification is the very reason we always desire something new and exciting. Continuing to seek fulfilment and never finding it.

Because none of these activities bring the inner peace and personal happiness we need, many turn to a cause. Such as social reform, saving the environment, or some other purpose to work for. The sad reality is that the majority of people do not look for the true source of peace and tranquility. Many become involved in a "Don Quixotic" type movement of fighting windmills that more often than not are secular, anti-God illusions. There are many of these worthless groups and organizations in the good old U. S. of A., and they find a multitude of folks who agree with and support them.

Another sad and frightening aspect of these groups activities are the changes being promoted that are opposite to the ideals that made this country great. Socialistic in nature, subversive in presentation and operation, they are able to convince many that drastic change in our society is necessary and for the betterment of the "poor," the "middle-class," or the "common" people. This smells like "class action" warfare, or the "caste" system to me.

They start by denying Godly ideals any role in the decision making process. Teaching the theory of evoluion as "fact," which does away with creation by God, whereby we should no longer recognize this out-dated "mythology." Bring in all of the non-Biblical ideas of abortion, same-sex marriage, and the notion that man is a god unto himself. Atheism and agnosticism become increasingly influential in the way ideas are promoted and made into the laws of the land.

In our modern culture the word "God" has become a meaningless symbol representing an abstract being without any relevance, or "scientific" proof. After all, according to the worldly thinkers, there are many gods, so why should we prefer one over another?

It is this very thinking that has brought this nation into a state of flux. Doubting the true

God of the Bible, and even denying His existence altogether. Does this observation appear realistic, or has it even crossed your mind as to what is taking place in this country?

In the book of Matthew, chapter 13, verse 15, we find Jesus speaking these words, "For this people's heart is waxed gross, and their ears are dull of hearing, and their eyes they have closed; lest at any time they should see with their eyes, and hear with their ears, and should understand with their hearts, and should be converted, and I should heal them." And in this same book, chapter 15, verse 14, Jesus calles them, "blind leaders of the blind."

The Bible gives us the reason for this worldly mind-set, and also the cure if we want it. First Corinthians, chapter 2, verse 14, "But the natural man receiveth not the things of the Spirit of God: for they are foolishness unto him: neither can he know them, because they are spiritually discerned."

In reality, the carnal nature of mortal man does not want Spiritual advice because in many cases it is a detriment to their world view. Scripture also casts a light on the sin in a persons life, that makes one uncomfortable. This is one of the main reasons why people dipute Biblical doctrine, or try to change it to suit their own agenda. Especially those who use religion as a means of making money.

A person who is sincere in their belief in Christ will follow the plan found in Ephesians 4:14, "That we henceforth be no more children, tossed to and fro, and carried about with every wind of doctrine, by the sleight of men, and cunning craftiness, whereby they lie in wait to deceive."

In other words, when one accepts Christ as their personal Savior and Lord, it is our <u>duty</u> and <u>obligation</u> to become grounded in the truth of God's Word. We must be prepared to recognize deceptive theology when we are exposed to doctrine that is not based on Scripture. A good orator can be an eloquent speaker and very convincing. But, if they disrespect and twist the truth of God with a clever ingenuity of mental ability, they are nothing more than a deceiver. The true Christian has been instructed to scrupulously distinguish and avoid this type of person and their teaching.

This reminds me of that old saying, "if a person tells or hears a lie often enough, it becomes truth to them." We have been building up to answer the title of this chapter, "Is America Now An Athiest Nation?"

With all of the religious deception that prevails in this country, it is no wonder that people turn away from the true God of the Bible. There are some who honestly don't know what to believe. Then there are others who categorically deny Biblical doctrine altogether.

The anti-God crowd have skillfully accomplished the removal of God and Christ from our institutions of learning and are continuing the fight in all public areas where God has been or is still recognized. The despicable and conniving thing they are doing now is going after churches that still preach the true Gospel and standing on their Constitutional right of free speech.

Now, back to our title question. We must remember the well publicized case of Judge Roy Moore, who was the Chief Justice of the Alabama Supreme Court. He was removed from office for refusing to remove the engraved granite monument of the Ten Commandments from the court house where he conducted his duties.

The ruling by U. S. District Judge Myron Thompson was that the display of the stone containing the Ten Commandments is <u>illegal</u>.

Thompson said the central most important issue was this: "Can the State ackowledge God?" After asking the question, he went on to answer it, "no."

What is the big deal, you ask? The First Amenment of our Constitution clearly states, "Congress shall make no law respecting the establishment of religion....." Which simply means that Congress is forbidden to set up a state sponsored, or national religion. And Congress has never passed any such law. And no one can abridge our right to worship God as we choose. The display of the Ten Commandments in no way can be called the "establishment" of a certain religion. What the un-Godly want to do is get rid of the <u>moral implication</u> of these Commandments!

With his signed order, Judge Thompson made atheism the "religion," or law of the land. Because the second half of the establisment clause of the First Amendment reads, ".....or prohibiting the free exercise thereof." And Judge Thompson <u>did</u> prevent, and prohibit, the "free exercise thereof." So, unless this ruling is recinded, atheism is the "official" law of the land. Quite different from what our founding fathers had in mind for the United States of America.

Do you believe that it should be possible for any Judge to simply declare or make a decision that <u>anything</u> is either legal or illegal just because that is how <u>they</u> think? Well that certainly appears to be the case!

Atheist- a person who believes that there is no God. Does not believe in the existence of any God or supernatural diety; rejects religion of any form. No divine authority. Atheists are "free thinkers," believing that religion is incompatable with reason.

A very clear-cut meaning of the word, is it not? However, they are "religiously" adament about the <u>theory</u> of evolution as being <u>fact</u>! They claim that there is no proof of creation by God, but fail to recognize that science has never <u>proven</u> evolution with <u>any</u> shred of evidence what so ever!

These people go hand in hand with the "peace movement" crowd. Including a bunch of far-left college professors. And Hollywood movie people, such as Ed Asner, Sean Penn, Mike Farall, Jane Fonda, Martin Sheen, and Michall Moore; just to name a few.

This so-called "peace movement" has many allies in our Congress, most of whom are of the Democrat Party, which has been taken over by the "hate America" zealots. This is the type of people we now have governing our nation. This is not something that people really think about because they keep electing them into office. But that's the problem, many don't <u>think</u> or <u>care</u> anymore!

In reality, the "peace movement" has nothing to do with "peace." It's objective is to create anarchy and destroy Christianity along with patriotism. They are trashing our Judeo-Christian heritage and replacing it with atheistic socialism.

It seems to be the main objective of that treasonous organization, the A.C.L.U., to file lawsuits prohibiting any public expression of Christianity and to harass Christians at every opportunity. Conservitive churches are one of their main targets.

The A.C.L.U., along with another Christian hate group, Americans United for Separation of Church and State, are extremely active in their efforts to silence Godly activity and expression. This latter group is headed by the "Reverand" Barry Lynn. Who, by the way, has never been known to pastor a church; but he is an A.C.L.U. attorney.

These organizations have sent spies into select churches to document and tape-record sermons in order to trap pastors who they <u>think</u> are promoting certain political candidates; people who do not go along with their secular views. And threatening churches of having their tax-exempt status taken away.

All of these hate groups are strong supporters of homosexual marriage, late term abortion, so-called hate crime laws, human cloning, gun control, and the teaching of evolution in our schools. These Satan inspired fanatics are waging war on Christians by their strong opposition to Bible reading and prayer in schools and any other "public" property. And even the wearing of religious symbols is taboo to them.

Consequently, and this I firmly believe, the worst result of this insidious liberal, socialistic, atheistic, humanistic, and secular thinking has infiltrated and contaminated many of our modern day churches. Whose clergy no longer preach repentance and the need for salvation through Jesus Christ, the significance of His death on the cross, and His shed blood for our redemption from sin. Or to live a changed life by faith through the teaching of Holy Scripture. A "socisl gospel," caring only for the physical needs of the masses. Mainly through government intervention and the use of tax-payer money. No redemptive qualities or personal responsibility, but to only follow their hedonistic agenda and philosophy like a band of sheep.

This secular ideology has caused devastation not only to the church, but also our government and the population in general. Most people no longer turn to God for strength, wisdom, or guidance, and have become increasingly less self reliant.

This all boils down to the question, what has happened to change the course of the United States of America? First of all, the underlying truth is, the majority of people have turned their backs on the true God of the Bible. And this just may be an understatement, as we witness so much unrestrained violence being perpetrated against all things that are righteous. Being a news junkie, I find that each day brings more evidence of the depravity and evil that has befallen this nation, and the world for that matter. However our concern is mainly for what is happening in America, which at one time was considered a Christian nation, based on our founding.

Today, in a local supermarket, I happened to meet an old aquaintance I had not seen in quite some time. After the ususl greetings of how are you, and what have you been doing lately, he asked this question: Have you noticed how things have changed in this country since we were kids? He went on talkig about how trashy and immoral are the things we see and hear today. Now, I did not bring up the subject, but found it quite interesting that it was another person of my generation who was able to recognize that America has indeed changed in a way that is not for the better.

Turning away from God is the principal reason why our culture is in a downward spiral. The law of human nature is simply this: do away with what is good and righteous and it <u>will</u> be replaced with what is corrupt and evil.

Secondly, we see and hear of the degrading acts commited by politicians, by people working in government, in our schools, in the entertainment industry, in sports, in business, and in religious organizations. Plus all the crimes that take place among the general populace, many of which are not even reported to authorities.

Another note worthy event was when Democrat Congressman Keith Ellison, of Minnesota, the first Muslim member of Congress, used the Quran in the photo-op of his swearing-in ceremony; it was soon forgotten news. How quickly we forget!

Thirdly, and by far the most revealing aspect of a fallen culture is the fact that we accept these things without a word or a second thought. Immorality has become the norm, and righteousness is spurned and laughed at. Biblical truth has become spurious and illegitimate to our secular society.

Now to conclude this thought we must turn to Scripture, our ultimate source for truth and reality. Matthew 24: 9 through 12, Jesus speaking to His Desciples, "Then shall they deliver you up to be afflicted, and shall kill you: and ye shall be hated of all nations for my name's sake." 10- "And then shall many be offended, and shall betray one another, and shall hate one another." 11- "And many false prophets shall rise, and shall deceive many." 12- "And because iniquity shall abound, the love of many shall wax cold."

Second Timothy 3:13, "But evil men and seducers shall wax worse and worse, deceiving and being deceived.

As followers of Christ today, we can expect no less severe treatment from the world than how His Desciples were treated in their day. And only you, from deep down in your heart, with all the evidence at hand, can answer the question, has America finally become an atheist nation?

As a nation, our primary founding was based on freedom <u>of</u> religion, now we are seeing the consequences of freedom <u>from</u> religion! And, of course, the "religion" we are being "set free" from is <u>Christianity</u>.

Chapter Eight

A Well Traveled Thouroghfare

In the book of Matthew, in the New Testament, chapter 7, verse 13, we find an admonition from Jesus, telling us this: "Enter ye in at the strait gate: for wide is the gate, and broad is the way, that leadeth to destruction, and <u>many</u> there be which go in thereat:"

Our primary focus will be on the last part of this verse, "and <u>many</u> there be which go in thereat." Along with that comes the question, why are so many headed for destruction?

If one is a devout student of the Bible and takes the time to <u>study</u> what is written therein, the answer is obvious. But for those who do not, and those who utterly reject the Word of God, allow me to offer a bit of explanation. This is not only from my perspective, through observation, but more importantly, from the pages of the Living Word.

First of all, man, in his natural, and mortal state of being, is <u>corrupt</u>. Is that being plain-spoken enough? There should be no misunderstanding on this point. Because there are many verses of Scripture that verify this statement. That is if you believe what the Bible teaches, and I do!

I will furnish references to read if you are at all curious, or if you dare expose yourself to the truth. Read Genesis 6: 11 and 12, Galatians 3:22, First John 1:8, and Romans 3:10 through 18. I prefer that you read these verses from the Bible yourself, so you might receive the full impact of what is written.

These verses are but a small sample of the "why" many people are traveling on the road that leads to destruction. If this was not the case, why would there be a need for God to provide a way of salvation? Good question! Oh, but perhaps you don't feel that there is a need? And that may be altogether true, if you have seared that still small voice within called your "conscience."

That little three letter word called "sin," is the culprit. And that is the real nature of mankind, hence the need for a Redeemer. The allure and deceitfulness of the world is very powerful and we cannot overcome this complex and compelling force in our own strength. You must understand that a person cannot win this battle alone.

Because of our worldly nature we are attracted to things that please our lusts and desires, fascinated and tempted to that which is unseemly. Is this God's doing? Absolutely not! We are enticed by our own will. In Matthew 26:41, Jesus said, "Watch and pray, that ye enter not into temptation: the spirit indeed is willing, but the flesh is weak."

It is this weakness of the flesh that Satan uses to turn mankind away from God. Romans 8:10, "And if Christ be in you, the body is dead because if sin; but the Spirit is life because of righteousness."

So, what is the outcome of our deliberate disregard of Godly instruction? Hebrews 10:26 and 27, gives us the answer, "For if we sin willfully after that we have received the knowledge of the truth, there remaineth no more sacrifice for sins," 27- "But a certain fearful looking for of judgment and fiery indignation, which shall devour the adversaries."

And just who are these "adversaries?" All of those who oppose the True God of the Bible and corrupt His Word with their own doctrine.

Sad to say, but <u>many</u> are traveling this broad road leading to eternal damnation. Some vehemently and deliberately rejecting anything that has to do with God or Christianity. The level of hatred directed against what is righteous is beyond a doubt Satan driven.

On the other hand, there are those who are marching down this road not fully aware of where they are going. It is this segment of the population that the Spirit of God will deal with, trying to bring about conversion through repentance and faith in Jesus Christ as their Savior and Lord. Yes, God is still at work trying to convince anyone who will hear the fact that eternity is real, and the choice of destination is a personal matter.

The question that might be asked is, how did this once great Christian nation change course? So let's examine three portions of Scripture that will shed some light on this question.

We will begin with First Timothy, chapter 4, verses 1 and 2, "Now the Spirit speaketh expressly, that in the latter times some shall depart from the faith, giving heed to seducing spirits, and doctrines of devils." 2- "Speaking lies in hypocrisy; having their conscience seared with a hot iron;"

Even some who once followed Christ will turn back into sin and the ways of the world. The Apostle Paul makes it clear that they will be seduced by evil and the teachings of devils, or men who are sold out to Satan. Speaking lies in deception because their conscience has been deadened, or made callous and unfeeling; hardened of heart.

Next on the list is Second Timothy, chapter 3, verses 1 through 5, also from the Apostle Paul, "This know also, that in the last days perilous times shall come." 2- "For men shall be lovers of their own selves, covetous, boasters, proud, blasphemers, disobedient to parents, unthankful, unholy," 3- "Without natural affection, truce-breakers, false accusers, incontinent, fierce, despisers of those that are good," 4- "Traitors, heady, highminded, lovers of pleasures more than lovers of God;" 5- "Having a form of Godliness, but denying the power thereof: <u>from such turn away</u>."

This is a precise description of our world today. And , as a nation, the United States of America has fallen into this category. We could look at each item of wrong doing that is on this list and recognize that they are epidemic accorss the country. The reason? Because many have failed to heed the advice of these four little words, "from such turn away."

The third item on our short list is Second Thessalonians, chapter 2, verses 10 through 12, once again, by the Apostle Paul, "And with all deceivableness of unrighteousness in them that perish; because they received not the love of the truth, that they might be saved." 11- "And for this cause God shall send them strong delusion, that they should believe a lie:" 12- "That they all might be damned who believed not the truth, but had pleasure in unrighteousness." And yes, if this sounds familiar it is because Scripture must be repeated over and over again until it sinks in.

Now I ask this question, where do most people find their pleasure? A simple observation of individuals and their priorities answers this question.

Every day we all make choices. Do we seek the things in life that are good, noble, and holy? Or do we have a tendency to go the other way? And when we decide on an important issue, do we follow Godly principles or, without thinking, simply give in to our lustful desires? Proverbs 14:12 should jolt us into reality, "There is a way which seemeth right unto a man, but the end thereof are the ways of death."

There are many things that happen in life that we look at as being beyond our control. As we watch and read the daily news reports we learn of many unusual and severe events that occur around the world. So we ask, what will be the next catastrophe that takes place, and where will it happen? I have read a report that the number of significant earthquakes has grown at an astonishing rate during the past ten to fifteen year period. Comparable to what has taken place in the preceding one hundred year time frame, and increasing in number each year.The same holds true for volcanic activity, tornadoes, hurricanes, flooding, and local severe thunderstorms with large hail and high winds.

What is happening with weather patterns to cause such destruction, injury, and death? An increasing number of people are jumping on the global warming bandwagon as being the reason.

Oh yes, let's not forget, according to "scientists" this is all due to "man-caused" climate change. This is all very strange to me because Germany's Institute of Marine Scientists say that we are in for a ten year period of global "cooling." There are <u>many</u> scientists, and by the report that I have read the number is <u>30,000</u>, yes that's thousands, who have signed a document stating a belief that there is no "settled science" as to "man-caused" global warming. This may be the mantra of Al Gore, the United Nations globalists, and a few others, but it is by <u>no</u> means a "settled or proven" scientific fact. It is amazing that people can be so gullible!

Even if there is global warming, I strongly disagree with the idea that it is caused by man. Just how much power does mortal man think we have in order to affect and "change" weather patterns? The very idea is idiotic! On the other hand, perhaps God allows weather events to effect a "change" in sinful mankind. Make no mistake about it, God alone is completely in control of the atmosphere and the elements of nature. And why God allows things to happen is entirely up to Him! To believe otherwise simply shows disbeleif, foolishness, and rejection of God's power and authority.

Matthew 24: 6 through 8, "And ye shall hear of wars and rumours of wars: see that ye be not troubled: for all these things must come to pass, but the end is not yet." 7- "For nation shall rise against nation, and kingdom against kingdom: and there shall be famines, and pestilences, and earthquakes, in divers places." 8- "All these are the beginning of sorrows."

Of course, I understand that many haughtily disagree and utterly reject anything that comes from the Bible. Even some who claim to be a Christian are skeptical and uncertain that Scripture means <u>exactly</u> what it is saying. Yes, I know, there are parables and similarities used in Scripture, but they are pointed out as being just that, a comparison of a certain situation.

My next statement will be very controversial, but here it is anyway. Those who doubt the authenticity and accuracy of the Bible are in the process of hardening their heart and becoming apostate to the truth of God's Word.

Hebrews 3:13, "But exhort one another daily, while it is called Today; lest any of you be hardened through the deceitfulness of sin." And the Bible is very clear, that to <u>doubt</u> what God says, through

His Word, is definitely sin. Doubt has the ability to kill one's faith in God.

Along this same thought, I would like to add another verse of Scripture that should be examined. First Peter 4:17. "For the time is come that judgment must begin at the house of God: and if it first begin at us, what shall the end be of them that obey not the Gospel of God?" A very startling question, is it not?

This clearly tells me that those of us who claim to be "Christian," must take a close look at our own life. Do we measure up to Biblical standards? Or do we simply follow along with the crowd that is traveling the "broad road?" It is easy to think in a self-righteous way and excuse our own behavior as long as we are "good citizens" and contribute time and money towards civic causes. This does not cut it as far as God is concerned! He accepts nothing less than our repentence from personal sin.

As one who believes Scripture to be the infallible Word of God, and every word that Crist Jesus had spoken to be profound, there is one short verse of great significance for our time. In Luke 5:32, Jesus said this, "I came not to call the righteous, but sinners to repentance."

If I read my Bible correctly, we <u>all</u> fall under the category of being a "sinner." Romans 3:10, "As it is written, There is none righteous, no, not one." Now the question arises, just what does it take to be a "true believer?" Once again, we go to Jesus for the answer. Luke 9:23, "And He said to them all, If any man will come after me, let him deny himself, and take up his cross daily, and follow me."

This is where the rubber meets the road. First of all, He tells us that <u>if</u> any man, and this is not gender specific but applies to both male and female, will follow after Him, certain criteria must be met.

I have heard discussions and sermons on the rest of this verse but never really gave it the credibility it deserves. It boils down to the root cause of why <u>many</u> are traveling the broad road to destruction.

This gets very personal when Christ tells us to <u>deny</u> ourselves, but we fail to understand just what this means. Simply put, I believe that <u>everything</u> we say and do must comply with Biblical instruction. On a daily basis, not just when we "feel" like it, or when someone is watching us, because as a Christian the Lord Jesus must be pre-eminent in our life.

How does one go about doing this? First of all it is imperitive to know what God has to say,and His instructions are found <u>only</u> in the Bible. An excellent example is James 1:21, "Wherefore lay apart all filthiness and superfluity of naughtiness, and receive with meekness the engrafted word, which is able to save your souls." The main ingredient that a Christian <u>must</u> posess is a "faith" in God. Romans 10:17, "So then faith cometh by hearing, and hearing by the Word of God." The point I want to make is this- life begins and ends by the unchanging Word of Almighty God. At this juncture I could go into any number of specifics, what to do or not to do, but it is <u>imperative</u> for a person to accept the urging of that "still small voice" from within, to repent of our sin. This is crucial, because God does not force Himself upon anyone. It is essential for one to come <u>willingly</u> to God, through His Son, Jesus Christ, in order to attain eternal life. This is when "faith" comes into effect, as an unquestioning belief in God. As a requisite to make this happen we read Hebrews 11:6, "But without faith it is impossible to please Him: for he that cometh to God must believe that He is, and that He is a rewarder of them that diligently seek Him."

Next question, how does one obtain faith? Faith is not something we are born with, nor does it just happen naturally. Faith is acquired, so one must put forth an effort to have it. The dictionary describes effort as the exertion, or using, of strength or mental power. Read again, Romans 10:17.

First John 5:4, "For whatsoever is born of God overcometh the world: and this is the victory that overcometh the world, even our faith." The Gospel of John, chapter5, verse 25, Jesus speaking, "Verily, verily, I say unto you, The hour is coming, and now is, when the dead shall hear the voice of the Son of God: and they that hear shall live."

There you have it. Our mortal being is Spiritually dead unless it is re-born through faith in Christ, which <u>only</u> comes about through the Written Word of God, the Bible. The majority of people do not even read the Bible, except perhaps for a few select verses that they use to appease their conscience.

There are two pertinent facts at play here. Number one: everyone, because of our carnal nature, are <u>spiritually</u> dead beings. Number two: each individual has the <u>choice</u> to either accept or reject life.

This is not something I have invented through my own imagination, nor have I pulled it out of thin air by some kind of magic trick. No, I could not conceive in my most wild dreams Gods plan of salvation, and how it must be attained . But this much I do know, it is written in "The Book," and I believe it with all of my heart. Does this make me special? Yes, and no. Because of this assurance, I have the hope of eternal life, yet, anyone can have the same confidence if they so choose. God is an equal opportunity provider!

The evidence that the United States is traveling down this broad road is overwhelming. Many of our laws are contrary to Judeo-Christian belief. Judges are allowed to interpret law according to their personal philosophy, while ignoring the will of the majority. Pagan worship is on the increase and given as much, or more, credibility as Christianity. Vulgarity has become the norm in our every day conversation, in personal speech, broadcast over the air-waves, and in print. Sexuality is explicit in many ways, including perverse homosexaul behavior, rampant sexually transmitted diseases, promiscuity, infidelity, and co-habiting without the obligation of marriage. I could go on and on, but I think you get the picture.

Our institutes of higher education are cesspools of anti-God teaching, with a very secular and socialistic agenda. Claiming to be broad minded but will not allow opposing opinions to even be discussed. Yet they like to teach certain theory as fact because it fits into their ideology. Everything must be politically correct and "tolerance" is their byword. Except they show no tolerance whatsoever to anyone with a Christian belief.

So, is there anyone out there sounding the alarm that this nation is sinking into a moral morass? Very few, and they are usually put down and told to shut up.

Have you ever seen Christianity and righteousness denigrated and mocked as often as it is today? I don't think so! At least I haven't in my lifetime. It has only become more blatant.

This is human nature without the influence of a Holy God. The doing away with what is right is <u>always</u> replaced with what is wrong. I assume that many would call this "freedom of expression." Tell that to God when you stand before Him in judgment. The humanistic secularists say there is no God and there is no judgment, so what do I have to worry about?

Now they have these questions to answer: why are you so aggressively and violently opposed to the God of the Bible if there is no such entity? Why do you fear and hate those that do have a belief in God? Good questions!

It is no secret, if we take the time to open our eyes, why the broad road to destruction is a well traveled highway, and becoming more crowded each day.

First and foremost, in my humble opinion, is the growing failure of the church to sound a warning. Ezekiel, chapter 33, verses 8 and 9, still apply to everyone claiming to be a Christian, and it is the express responsibility of the clergy. "When I say unto the wicked, O wicked man, thou shalt surely die: if thou dost not speak to warn the wicked man from his way, that wicked man shall die in his iniquity: but his blood will I require at thine hand." 9- "Nevertheless, if thou warn the wicked of his way to turn from it; if he do not turn from his way, he shall die in his iniquity; but thou hast delivered thy soul."

This portion of Scripture was taken from the Standard King James translation, but since this has such great significance we will also share the New International Version of these same verses.

Perhaps this will give a little more clarification. "When I say to the wicked, O wicked man, you will surely die, and you do not speak out to dissuade him from his ways, that wicked man will die for his sin, and I will hold you accountable for his blood." 9- "But if you do warn the wicked man to turn from his ways and he does not do so, he will die for his sin, but you will have saved yourself."

Christianity carries a tremendous responsibility, but many have the fear of offending people if they mention the consequences of sin. This does not require a Christian to shove their ideology down anyone's throat. We have a good example in Isaiah 1:18, "Come now, let us reason together, saith the Lord: though your sins be as scarlet, they shall be as white as snow; though they be red like crimson, they shall be as wool."

This tells me that God is reasonable, and will guide us with patience, love, and mercy, if we are willing to listen. Second Timothy 2: 24 through 26, "And the servant of the Lord must not strive; but be gentle unto all men, apt to teach, patient," 25- "In meekness instructing those that oppose themselves; if God peradventure will give them repentance to the acknowledging of the truth;" 26- "And that they may recover themselves out of the snare of the devil, who are taken captive by him at his will."

There you have it in a nutshell. However, this by no means is to imply that Christians are weak-kneed wimps! It takes courage, perseverance, a back-bone, determination, and the desire to please God, if one is to take a stand for, and embrace, righteousness. Not having all of these characteristics is the very reason why many in the clergy are actually on the "broad road."

I have some strong words for all of us "common" folks as well. When we ignore, or turn aside from God's direction in our life we become slothful, indifferent, careless, and complacent. Our attitude and actions can cause a multitude of traffic on the road to destruction. This is a very somber thought; to actually be the cause of someone losing their soul for all eternity.

What really amazes me is that _many_ professing "Christians" don't even read and study the Bible on a regular basis. How can this be? How else can we become acquainted with our Lord? And if those who claim to be of this faith fail to be diligent in their pursuit of "knowing God," what can we expect from others who outright deny the existence of God, or who simply believe that God is not relevant in their daily life? We, as Christians, can allow ourselves to become lazy and careless in the way we treat the Word of God. Through neglect and the cares of <u>this</u> life, we often put the responsibility of securing the <u>next</u> life on the back burner, or forget about it altogether. And, if our "urgent" requests, or prayers, are not answered immediately, or to our satisfaction, we question God's ability, or doubt that He even cares. Often we will feel sorry for ourselves and have a little "pity party." Remember this: without <u>faith</u> we cannot please God, and faith comes through <u>His Word</u>! As for anti-Christians, they show no interest or need for Biblical doctrine. They are self-satisfied and self-righteous, considering themselves to be neutral about "religion;" unconcerned and completely apathetic. Considering the Word of God to be of no consequence, and unimportant. Convinced in their own mind, and so smug in their worldly status to the point that nothing else matters. The road to destruction is broad and well traveled. Are you on this highway?

Chapter Nine
Straight And Narrow

In the preceding chapter, we discussed the broad road to destruction. Now, we will go back to Matthew chapter 7, verse 14, "Because strait is the gate, and narrow is the way, which leadeth unto life, and few there be that find it." This is in absolute contrast to the "broad road."

Now this bothers me a great deal, and should be a concern for every Christian. Not only for our own well being, but also for our loved ones, and any we are able to influence.

If only we would realize that this is a matter of a spiritual "life and death," which is eternal, just maybe, more people will wake up to reality.When we approach the subject of "eternity," it kind of blows our mind. It is difficult to get a handle on this word and it's meaning. A continuance <u>without end</u>, infinite time, time without beginning or end. I know that in the finite mind and reasoning of a mortal being, this is almost impossible to understand.

In the book of Isaiah, chapter 57, verse 15, we are told this about God, "For thus saith the high and lofty One that inhabiteth eternity, whose name is Holy; I dwell in the high and holy place, with him also that is of a contrite and humble spirit, to revive the spirit of the humble, and to revive the heart of the contrite ones."

This is one tough verse of Scripture for anyone to get the full meaning of, and especially for non-believers. It does, however, reveal that "eternity" is God's dwelling place. A real "somewhere," if I may use that term.

Psalm 90:2, "Before the mountains were brought forth, or ever thou hadst formed the earth and the world, even from everlasting to everlasting, thou art God."

Eternity is everlasting, forever! Rather hard to imagine, is it not? Perhaps this is the reason why few are able to find the "strait and narrow way."

It was about a year ago I felt that God, through the Holy Spirit, had impressed upon my mind these two particular verses of Scripture, Matthew 7:13 and 14. The explicit meaning of what Jesus relates to us is very sobering. You don't hear a great deal of commentary from preachers anymore on this subject, "the many and the few." The more I study the Bible, and take note of current events, the more I realized how serious the problem of agnosticism in America has become.

Searching for cause, I was directed to the book of Second Timothy, chapter 3. In this portion of Scripture, we are given a list of vices that are an entrapment in the lives of many.

The factors that stand out in my mind concerning this particular writing are three-fold. Number one- we are told to know this also, "that in the last days perilous times shall come." Number two- "that men shall be lovers of their own selves." And number three, which is the epitome of our modern culture- "that men shall be lovers of pleasure more than lovers of God."

I know that it is extremely difficult for us to imagine the "last days." And for many it is simply a myth thought up by religious zealots. Even for Christians who are enjoying a good life, this subject is kind of passed over and thought of as something in the distant future.

When I think of the "last days," it is in reality a two-sided coin. The Biblical "last days" may, or may not, be in the process of development, I do not know. However, the signs of prophesy seem to be pointing in that direction. Nevertheless, who among us know for certain when their earthly "last day" will occur? At the death of our mortal body, it will be the end of our days on earth. This is <u>proven fact</u>! In either case one must be prepared for what comes next.

According to the Bible, the "last days" speak of a time of great suffering and many catastrophic events taking place all over the world. A person has to be blind, or terribly naïve not to see the devestation caused by severe "acts of nature." Add to this secnario the violence of man against man. It is easy to see that this world is in a problematic time.

The vast majority of people are just waiting and hoping for things to get better, Many believe that the "right person" will come along and straighten out all of our difficulties.

The politicians tell us that if only we elect this man or that woman, to change the way our government functions, it will solve all of our problems. Yes, and I have a bridge over a large river in the Sahara Desert that I will sell real cheap!

Without God, man is unable to solve problems of great proportion, but will only cause complications. And the farther we are removed from God, the worse our condition becomes. Remember how relatively simple life was in days gone by, compared to our modern day life style? We are over-taxed, over-regulated, and overworked, which only adds more pressure to our already hetic way of living. And besides, "we ain't gonna be out-done by our friends and neighbors!" I think of this as the "spoiled brat attitude."

The United States has become increasingly more socialistic in the desire for government to take care of our every need. This has been a failure in all other countries and will fail here as well. This nation was a democratic republic, with power vested in the hands of "we the people." Technically, this is no longer the case. We are living under a socialistic pattern of law, or government, that has taken over the production and distribution of goods and services to the people. There is absolutely no type of business, organization, or private entity in this nation, that is not governed by a law or regulation. Socialized medicine is the buzz-word for all of our political and intellectual nabobs. Even though they may not use that particular terminology. Take from the rich and give to the poor! Only it doesn't work that way. We will end up with the masses being ruled by an elite few. Check out world history and see if that is not the case. Do you say this can't happen in the good old U.S. of A.? Well I have news for you my friend. It is a sly and insidious ideology that is being promoted in an incremental manner by our very own government. Slowly, but surely, America has reached this state of being, duped into a system that will bring about our downfall as a great nation.

If you doubt what I am saying, please, explain to me, in an understandable and precise way, how we will attain the lofty goals promised by all of these smart folks who are running, and would like to run, the affairs of this country?

They are smooth talkers, whose only goal is to gain power and control over the "common" people. Their promises sound good and appeal to many who are looking for something for nothing, but the only way to make it happen is to <u>take</u> from the working folks and businesses, and let the government do the distribution. Two big problems come with that idea. Number one is, the governments portion is <u>always</u> the largest share. Number two, the government only gives a very little to those it considers worthy of it's benevolence. How else can it get bigger to do more good? Give me a break!

Oh yes, another strange thing happened awhile back, during our rush to insanity. A well-known pastor from the Midwest was chastised by one of the presidential candidates, for calling Islam an evil religion. O.k., if the main holy book of this "religion" <u>orders</u> the death of <u>all</u> who do not convert, or believe in their faith, what do you call it, other than evil? Good question! This reminds me of what is written in the first part of Romans 1:25, speaking of those who subvert the Word of God, it states, "who changed the truth of God into a lie...."

Shall we dig a little deeper into the character of those who want to rule over this nation, and reject the truth of God as being of no cosquence?

Yes, we will go to the "Living Word" for an apt description.

Psalm 36: 1 through 4, (the NIV translation) "An oracle is within my heart concerning the sinfulness of the wicked: There is no fear of God before his eyes." 2- "For in his own eyes he flatters himself too much to detect or hate his sin." 3- "The words of his mouth are wicked and deceitful; he has ceased to be wise and to do good." 4- "Even on his bed he plots evil; he commits himself to a sinful course and does not reject what is wrong."

The one who penned this Psalm used some very strong and pointed language, detailing the thoughts and actions of those who are wicked. First of all, in the heart of these individuals, they see no reason to fear God. Then they go on to flatter and self-delude themselves into believing they really are something. They commit unjust acts with hatred, perpetrated against anyone not in agreement with them. The words of their mouth are unrighteous and deceitful, unwilling to seek wisdom to do what is good. We are told that they lay in bed at night scheming more wicked deeds, setting themselves on a course that is malicious and immoral They do not hate unrighteousness, but rather promote more evil!

We will continue on, to shed a little more light on the distinguishing traits of those who choose to disregard Biblical instruction.

Proverbs 6: 16 through 19, (NIV translation) "There are six things the Lord hates, seven that are detestable to Him:" 17- "Haughty eyes, a lying tongue, hands that shed innocent blood," 18- "A heart that devises wicked schemes, feet that are quick to rush into evil," 19- "A false witness who pours out lies and a man who stirs up dissention among brothers."

This portion of Scripture is precise, very clear and to the point, needing no further clarification from me. However, I will say this, that it describes a pattern of conduct we find all too often in many of the "leaders" we have today .

There is also a verse of Scripture found in Second Corinthians 10:12, that I will bring to your attention, "For we dare not make ourselves of the number, or compare ourselves with some that commend themselves: but they measuring themselves by themselves, and comparing themselves among themselves, are not wise." Read this verse a few times and let it sink in. Self-agrandizement is the trait described here. Is this not a characteristic of many high-profile individuals who want to run the country and control the lives of others? Think about it!

One more verse of wisdom that everyone, especially Christians, should consider when looking at people who claim to have all the answers for the problems besetting this nation. Colossians 2:8 "Beware lest any man spoil you through philosophy and vain deceit, after the tradition of men, after the rudiments of the world, and not after Christ."

This really puts a damper on the lofty and vain claims of people who promise great things and and at the same time ignore and disavow Gods commandments and the teaching of Jesus, our Lord and redeemer. The United States of America is speeding through familiar territory, and this road is certainly not the straight and narrow way.

So, is character important? Do we qualify people by their history of past performance, or by their cunning and deceitful rhetoric of promises they cannot and do not plan to keep?

When people who are in power deliberately and knowingly reject the teaching of Holy Scripture as being undoable, unacceptable, and unnecessary, we as a nation will suffer the consequences. When our leaders condone and fraternize with those who promote a life-style of sin and debauchery, this country is headed down the wrong road.

We are constantly hearing that this nation needs to change course. Truer words have never been spoken! The only problem is, that those seeking the power and authority to make change, are wanting to take us from a bad situation to one that is even worse.

Just what do I mean by this last statement? Well, we are already in a moral morass of bewilderment that has no precedent, except for one other time in history. Believe it or not, but the Bible has a record of such a time.

In Genesis, the first book of the Bible, after God had created man, and after the fall of Adam and Eve, the population of the earth began to multiply rapidly. In the fifth chapter of this book, we are introduced to a man named Noah. Yes, this is an old story that many are familiar with. And which many discount as being mythology. Noah, and the flood that covered the earth, is impossible for the atheists, secularist, and like minded folks, to accept as fact. However, they do, and very religiously I might add, believe the earth and mankind "evolved" from <u>nothing</u>! Talk abount impossible; just how intelligent is that idea? We could debate this until the end of time, which is another subject, but we will go on to the real purpose of this narrative.

Genesis 6: 5 through 8, "And God saw that the wickedness of man was great in the earth, and that every imagination of the thoughts of his heart was only evil continually." 6- "And it repented the Lord that He had made man on the earth, and it grieved Him at His heart." 7- "And the Lord said, I will destroy man whom I have created from the face of the earth; both man and beast, and the creeping thing, and the fowls of the air; for it repenteth me that I have made them." 8- "But Noah found grace in the eyes of the Lord."

Two verses of this short portian of Scripture stand out. The fifth and eighth verses are of a contrasting nature. The fifth verse gives us a picture, or description, of man in his depravity at it's highest level. What else could cause so much vexation for God to destroy His human and animal creation?

When every thought and imagination in the heart of mankind was <u>continually</u> evil, that is something very difficult to comprehend. But it does give us an inkling of how base and degenerate people can become once they forsake God and His law, or commandments.

As for the flood to have actually happened, the fossil record is clear and understandable, to anyone with the brain power of truth and reason. Admittedly, I am an amature paleontologist, however, I have discovered for myself many fossilized aquatic creatures on the very tops of high hills in what can only be described as desolate, and barron countryside. Far away from any body of water from which these creatures originated. There is only one way that these fossils could possibly have been placed where they were found. So you have to decide in your own mind if the flood of Noah's day was a reality.

For a confirmation of the truth concerning Noah, we will look at what Jesus had to say about this matter. For the true born-again believer, it is a readily understood and accepted theology. But for those who doubt what the Bible teaches, at some point in time, you will have to make a decision one way or the other, to accept or reject the truth of Scripture.

In the Gospel of Matthew, chapter 24, verses 37 through 39, Christ Jesus tells us this, "But as the days of Noah were, so shall also the coming of the Son of Man be." 38- "For as in the days that were before the flood they were eating and drinking, marrying and giving in marriage, until the day that Noah entered into the ark," 39- "And knew not until the flood came, and took them all away; so shall also the coming of the Son of Man be."

In comparing the time of Noah to our present day, it is exactly the same as far as culture is concerned. Of course we have all of the modern conveniences that were not available then, however we are speaking of conditions of the heart, and how we view morality according to God's Word. Life is going on as it was in Noah's day, with sin and evil every bit as rampant, spreading unchecked and uncontrolled.

It makes no difference how many laws are passed, for or against something, people are going to do what is in their heart and mind. Many say that we cannot legislate morality, but that is a lie, dreamed up by those with a secularist world view. On the contrary, our laws, according to the Constitution, are moral laws! But, they have been changed by individuals to suit their own agenda, or so-called "political correctness." It is amazing that our government is afraid that Christians will offend someone by saying, doing, and being what God expects them to say, do, and be, if it is in a "public" place.Talk about discrimination, this is it!

Jesus also has something to say for the "climate change" advocates, and the environmental zealots. Luke 21: 25 and 26, "And there shall be signs in the sun, and in the moon, and in the stars; and upon the earth distress of nations, with perplexity; the sea and the waves roaring;" 26- "Mens hearts failing them for fear, and, for looking after those things which are coming on the earth: for the powers of heaven shall be shaken."

Events are taking place in the world that man cannot explain or understand. So they rush about touting some <u>theory</u> they believe is fact. Perplexed, and totally confused, they call for change and hope, only to be unclear as to what should be changed or what to hope for.

What kind of "change" are people looking for? The worldly thinkers have already changed the truth of God's Word into lies, and worshipping things and creatures rather than God. Exchanging Godly behavior for conduct that is abominable, making perversion and all manner of sin acceptable. Mocking and shameing those who dare to stand up for what is right. The big problems are that the "changes" taking place, and being considered, are not for the good of the people.

And hope? Just what and who do we place our hope in? Some person with empty promises? Or "things" we strive to acquire? Proverbs 26:12, "Seest thou a man wise in his own conceit? There is more hope of a fool than of him." And also Proverbs 29:20, "Seest thou a man that is hasty in his words? There is more hope of a fool than of him."

Once again we look at what Jesus said; Luke 12:15, "And He said unto them, Take heed, and beware of covetousness: for a mans life consisteth not in the abundance of the things which he possesseth."

In Colossians 3:2, we find this admonition, "Set your affection on things above, not on things on the earth."

Now for the bottom line of hope, the essence of what hope really is, Titus 3:7, "That being justified by His grace, we should be made heirs according to the <u>hope</u> of eternal life."

This is where we come into conflict with the world. Our hope, that of a Christian, is based entirely on the promises of Christ, through faith in His Word. Hope in anything or anyone else is futile, without the guidance of our Holy God.

But of course the world will have none of Him, consequently, they find themselves falling deeper into the pit of sin and evil doing, finding nothing but remorse and hopelessness.

Let's get back to the "narrow way" and the few there be who find it. I want you to notice that this is a way that must be <u>found</u>. Because of our mortal, sinful nature, the narrow way is not readily seen or understood.

Many believe that doing good deeds, acting piously, or belonging to some religious group, is going to assure one of a heavenly future. Some folks believe that there are many entrances into heaven. Not so! People can rant and rave and claim bigotry all they want, but <u>only</u> through faith in Jesus Christ as our personal Savior and Lord of one's life, can this be accomplished, by the cleansing power of His shed Blood, on the cross at Calvary. THERE IS NO OTHER WAY! We can find much Scripture that will verify this fact, but I will quote only one verse for you to meditate upon, John." 14:6, "Jesus saith unto him, (speaking to His desciple, Thomas), "I am the way, the truth, and the life: no man cometh unto the Father, but by Me."

Yes, I understand, for a great many this is entirely unreasonable, and not something that a "loving God" would require. But remember, it is God who provided this means of salvation for mankind, and we have the choice to accept it or not. Also remember, God allowed His Son to be sacrificed for our redemption.

Do mere human beings dictate to God Almighty, who created us in the first place? Sorry, all of you evolutionists, you are definitely not on the "straight and narrow way." And I don't have to prove anything! Just being able to see the beauty, the magnificence, and the orderliness of the universe, is proof enough for me.

Psalm 19: 1 through 4, "The heavens declare the glory of God; and the firmament sheweth His handiwork." 2- "Day unto day uttereth speech, and night unto night sheweth knowledge." 3- "There is no speech nor language, where their voice is not heard." 4- "Their line is gone out through all the earth, and their words to the end of the world. In them He set a tabernacle for the sun."

The very heavens and earth reveal the glory of our heavenly Father. God has set the pattern of day and night, and through His creation we receive knowledge of Him. There is no place nor language where this cannot be seen and understood, for His glory encompasses the entire world. And He put the sun in it's place for His purpose and our benefit.

Lets go to the seventh verse of this same chapter. One of the most profound and beautiful verses of Scripture. "The law of the Lord is perfect, converting the soul: the testimony of the Lord is sure, making wise the simple."

If the law of God is perfection, able to convert the mortal into immortality, and His Word is sure, strong, and true, giving wisdom to the most simple mind, what more can we ask? But this must be <u>found</u>, and <u>accepted</u>,and <u>lived</u>, for the purpose of an everlasting eternity with Him. This is called <u>salvation!</u>

Salvation is so simple and reasonable, that it is a stumbling block to many, and does not meet their requirements or intellect.

Why is the "straight and narrow road" that leads to eternal life, less traveled than the "broad way" that leads to destruction? Of course it is easy to see what man determines as sin, such as murder, rape, drunkenness, theft, lying, etc., as being the main reason. However, unbelief is the prime offense that will keep a person from entering heaven.

Second Corinthians 4: 3 and 4, "But if our Gospel be hid, it is hid to them that are lost." 4- "In whom the god of this world hath blinded the minds of them which believe not,......." Next, Titus 1:15, "Unto the pure all things are pure: but unto them that are defiled and unbelieving is nothing pure; but even their mind and conscience is defiled." And thirdly, First John 5: 10 through 12, "He that believeth on the Son of God hath the witness in himself: he that believeth not God hath made Him a liar; because he believeth not the record that God gave of His Son." 11- "And this is the record, that God hath given to us eternal life, and this life is in His Son." 12- "He that hath the Son hath life; and he that hath not the Son of God hath not life."

These Scriptures are not difficult to understand, but are meaningless to all who harden their heart and refuse to accept the teaching of the Bible as infallible truth. We are free to choose what we <u>want</u> to believe, and God is free to choose what we <u>must</u> believe. First Corinthians 1: 25 through 29, "Because the foolishness of God is wiser than men; and the weakness of God is stronger than men." 26- "For ye see your calling, brethren, how that not many wise men after the flesh, not many mighty, not many noble, are called:" 27- "But God hath chosen the foolish things of the world to confound the wise; and God hath chosen the weak things of the world to confound the things which are mighty;" 28- "And base things of the world, and things which are despised, hath God chosen, yea, and things which are not, to bring to naught things that are:" 29- "That no flesh should glory in His presence."

Man, seeking the adulation of man, wanting praise and admiration heaped upon themselves, is a prominent vice among Christian "bashers." People looking for self-glory, or fame, want nothing to do with the commandments of a Holy God. They fall into the category of those who said, "Lord, Lord, have we not done great things in your name?" And He said unto them, "depart from me you workers of iniquity, for I know you not."

The truth of the matter is, we cannot fool or trick God. He understands the motive of our heart, and when we take glory that belongs to God, we are in deep trouble.

The fact that "few there be" who will find the "straight and narrow way," is simply because people turn their back on God and reject His "way" of life, following instead the deciet of this world, controlled by Satan.

This is a sad picture, and should cause us to examine our own life, to see if we measure up with what God expects of us. Sad, in the fact that everyone has the opportunity to receive eternal life, but are made blind by unbelief, the allure of sin for a season, following the dictates of the world, unable and unwilling to find the "straight and narrow road." Sad, in the fact that our mortal life is temporal, and eternity is endless, and more people will choose destruction rather than life.

Straight and narrow is the road, but "few there be that find it." How sad!

Chapter Ten

Why Christianity?

It is not for man to question why God works in a certain way. After all, He is God, the Creator of everything, the Almighty, the Everlasting God!

Here I go again, making statements that cannot be proven. Or, so say those who do not accept Biblical truth; and they are many.

That there has been a "beginning" of life is not in question. The argument is, just <u>how</u> did life begin? Of course the evolutionist, or world view, is the "big bang" theory. That <u>everything</u> evolved from <u>nothing</u>.

Now let's examine this word, "nothing," that many seem to have a problem with. It means non-existence, nothingness, a thing that does not exist, zero, having no implicating evidence.

To exist, there has to be "reality," or actual "being." Specific manifestation, an entity. A thing that has definite, individual existence in reality or in the mind; anything that is real. Wow! This is rocket science, right? Just kidding.

The manisfestation of the world and the universe is clear, palpable, we can see, touch, and feel it. Does this sound like "nothing?" How ridiculous! Yet, this fantastic, or fantasy, idea is swallowed hook line and sinker by the majority of people. Are we no longer capable of reason or sound thinking? Apparently not!

The word "delusion" comes to mind. We are mislead, or tricked, into believing a false idea, or an opinion, that is the complete opposite of reality. A persistant and false belief not substantiated by sensory or objective evidence. And believe me, the world is persistant in <u>demanding</u> that everyone accept this false "science" of evolution.

The Old Testament book of Isaiah, chapter 64, verse 4, tells us this, "For since the beginning of the world men have not heard, nor perceived by the ear, neither hath the eye seen, O God, beside thee, what He hath prepared for him that waited for Him."

Next, in chapter 66, verse 4, the prophet Isaiah is told this by God, "I also will choose their delusions, and will bring their fears upon them; because when I called, none did answer; when I spake, they did not hear: but they did evil before mine eyes, and chose that in which I delighted not."

For confirmation, we will review again what is written in the book of Second Thessalonians, chapter 2, verses 10 and 11, "And with all deceivableness of unrighteousness in them that perish; because they received not the love of the truth, that they might be saved." 11- "And for this cause God shall send them strong delusion, that they should believe a lie:"

What has this to do with Christianity? Well, it is God's plan of redemption that is being rejected, by all who refuse His truth. Since the beginning of time, the majority of people have refused to acknowledge the hand of God in "creation," even though it is easily seen. They have turned a deaf ear to what God is telling us through His Word and want no part of the truth of Scripture. God is very patient and long-suffering, allowing mankind plenty of time and opportunity to repent. But because of unbelief and hardness of heart, they continually refuse His love and mercy. This does not fully answer the question, "why Christianity?", but it does give us a foundation to build upon.

First of all, God knew the outcome of His human creation. Secondly, He placed within every person a free moral agency, or the <u>ability</u> to choose our own way of life. We are not robots, we are flesh and blood mortal beings. And I don't have the answer as to why God does things a certain way. Because I am but a small part of His creation, I must accept the fact that God <u>knows</u> what He is doing.

A created being does not have the authority, nor the power, to dictate what the Creator does. But it is in my own interest that I pay attention to what He says.

I cannot speak for everyone concerning a decision to accept Christ as their personal savior, and to follow Him; but only as the Lord relates to me. In Philippians, chapter 2, the last part of verse 12, the Apostle Paul gives us this advice, ".....work out your own salvation with fear and trembling." Salvation is not something to be taken lightly with a flippant or careless attitude, because God deserves our utmost respect and reverence. This is not to infer in any way that God is a hard task master, on the contrary, Christians serve the Lord with joy and gladness, living to please Him. After all, GOD is GOD! And we are His creation, made for His express purpose. That God would care enough about mankind to provide such a marvelous plan for our eternity simply boggles my mind. Human reasoning cannot fully understand this kind of love. There must be a "spiritual awakening" of our heart and mind to make salvation complete between God and man.

I was brought up in church and Sunday-school, but this did not constitute a "conversion," however, I do believe that is where the seed was planted to bring about the actual "change" in my life.

I am completely convinced that there is a "still small voice" inside each and every person born into this world, called a "conscience." To know God, one must become acquainted with "who" He is. The Bible is replete with the characteristics and descriptions of God, but I will make this portrayal very simple. God is of a triune, a three person trinity, or God-head. God the Father, God the Son, and God the Holy Spirit. Having the same mind and thought, yet working in their own separate capacity, with the exact same goal; complete unity. God also created man as a three part entity, body , soul, and spirit. And one function of God the Holy Spirit, is to communicate with man through his conscience; that "still small voice" we were born with.

It is a known fact that our body is a temporal thing and when death occurs it returns to dust, from which it was made. And the big question remains, what about the soul and spirit that once occupied that dead body?

But first, let's back-track for a moment, to get our ducks in a row. Genesis 2:7, "And the Lord God formed man of the dust of the ground, and breathed into his nostrils the breath of life; and man became a living soul." This was our beginning, created from a substance, the dust of the earth, not from evolution of "nothing,"which is an impossibility.

Ecclesiastes 12:7, "Then shall the dust return to the earth as it was: and the spirit shall return unto God who gave it." Ezekiel 18:4, God speaking to the prophet Ezekiel, "Behold, all souls are mine; as the soul of the father, so also the soul of the son is mine: the soul that sinneth, it shall die."

Hebrews 9:27, "And as it is appointed unto men once to die, but after this the judgment:" Now you have the cycle of the mortal being that God created. From our beginning to the ending of this human body.

The spirit and soul of man, I would consider to be that "breath of life" God breathed into the first man, Adam. And, at the physical death of this mortal body, they are reclaimed by God. Reserved until the day of judgment, when the righteous go to be with the Lord in His dwelling place, and the unrighteous into eternal punishment.

This is of course a simplified version, because there is much written about the two final places of eternity. God will create a new heaven and a new earth for the redeemed, while Satan, his angles, and all the occupants of Hell, and Hell itself, shall be cast into the Lake of Fire, the eternal abode of the damned.

Back to the question of "Why Christianity?", or the person professing belief in Jesus as Savior and Lord. Christianity is a collective group of people whose faith is based on the teaching of the Old and New Testaments, the Holy Bible.

It is a sorrowful and deplorable situation that there are those who subvert this Holy Book for their own personal gain, and turn it into a world-view philosophy. Twisting and destroying the true meaning of Holy Scripture to satisfy a sinful life style. The Bible warns us to stay away from unsound doctrine.

This brings up the next important question, what about all of the other religions and cults of the world? Is this not a valid and interesting question? Of course it is. We, as Christians, must have a good reason for what we believe.

As I have mentioned already, I do not know the circumstances concerning the conversion of others into the Christian faith. I can only speak for myself, because this is a very personal relationship between an individual and his God.

Did I experience an exaggerated feeling of euphoria when this life change happened? No. However I did have a vast sense of relief. As if I had done something of great importance, but unable to fully understand the consequence of what was taking place.

Over time, hearing others expound on Biblical teaching, but mostly through the study of Scripture on my own, this Book, the Bible, became an amazing source of knowledge. The road map to eternal life through faith in the Son of God!

Much too simple, you say? Yes it is, for those who believe that man, in his intellect, has all the answers of life. Or who believe that man is capable through science and technology to <u>find</u> the answers for all things.

But, what about spiritual matters that science and human intelligence cannot explain? This does not have any relevance, you say? How does one escape that "still small voice" inside of us that causes a person to think about life and death, and, is there really an "after-life?"

Try as we may, we cannot escape this burning question of, "is there actually <u>something</u> beyond this mortal life?" Yes, we can ignore these thoughts and claim adamantly that there is no such thing. But until one's conscience is seared, and their heart is hardened into unbelief, this question will not go away. You see, God , in all of His wisdom, and through the urging of the Holy Spirit, will not give up on an individual. God does all He can, without the use of force, to convince mankind that His way is the <u>right</u> way, and the <u>only</u> way.

It is man, by his own choice, when he turns his back on God and goes his own way, it will lead to eternal damnation. Don't blame God for what is your own decision.

In the book of Job, chapter 12, verse 10, speaking of God, we are told this, "In whose hand is the soul of every living thing, and the breath of all mankind."

Why choose Christianity? Because we <u>are</u> in God's hands, and the very breath of our life is dependant upon Him.

Psalm 49:15, "But God will redeem my soul from the power of the grave: for He shall receive me. Selah."

Why choose Christianity? Because the grave cannot keep us! We will be received into the presence of God. By the way, that word "Selah" is a Hebrew word used at the end of some verses in the Psalms, traditionally interpreted as a blessing, meaning "forever." This is great, is it not?

First Corinthians 15:45 through 47, "And so it is written, The first man Adam was made a living soul; The last Adam was made a quickening spirit." 46- "Howbeit that was not first which is spiritual, but that which is natural; and afterward that which is spiritual." 47- "The first man is of the earth, earthy: the second man is the Lord from Heaven." All human-kind are natural born descendants of the first man, Adam. All "Believers" are spiritually re-born through the Life, Death, and Resurrection of Jesus Christ.

Why choose Christianity? Because God has provided a way of salvation that has no equal proposal, nor anything that even comes close. In order to provide justification for the natural, or "earthly" man, God prepared His Son to be the propitiate, or appeaser, for sinful man to be reconciled to our Heavrnly Father.There is no other way to eternal life, period!

A person has to be blind, or completely ignorant, to not see the turmoil and chaos taking place in the world today. From human violence and depravity to what man calls "natural disasters" of huge proportions.

These things have been prophesied in Scripture to take place. To those who study God's Word, this is no surprise. But it sure has many worldly thinkers, from medical doctors, psychiatrists, and scientists, trying to come up with answers. At the same time, dismissing and rejecting Biblical prophesy as irrelevant or as mythological, and not to be considered practical or even possible.

This reminds me of the soothsayers and sorcerers that we read about in the Bible. When kings and rulers wanted answers to things they did not understand, this is who they called on for advice. But not on God, because they did not believe in Him. Does this sound familiar?

There are a few occasions recorded in Scripture when a ruler did seek the advice of a man of God. And when this did happen, they were always told the truth. If it was a prophesy of coming events, or a warning from God, it <u>always</u> came to pass, without exception. I could cite many accounts, but study the Bible for yourself to prove if this is true or not.

Why Christianity? Another reason is the value God has placed on the soul of man. Matthew 16:26, "For what is a man profited, if he shall gain the whole world, and lose his own soul? Or what shall a man give in exchange for his soul?"

Two very relevant questions. Because our soul is everlasting and bound for eternity, what good would it do to own the entire world when it is going to be destroyed anyway? Long ago, God gave us a glimpse into the future when He said this to the prophet Isaiah, "For, behold, I create new heavens and a new earth: and the former shall not be remembered, nor come into mind." Isaiah 65:17. And this from the prophet Zephaniah, Chapter 3, verse 8, "Therefore wait ye upon Me, saith the

Lord, until the day that I rise up to the prey: for my determination is to gather the nations, that I may assemble the kingdoms, to pour upon them mine indignation, even all my fierce anger: for all the earth shall be devoured with the fire of my jealousy."

Let's not stop with the Old Testament prophets, but proceed to the New Testament. Second Peter 3: 5 through 7, "For this they willingly are ignorant of, that by the Word of God the heavens were of old, and the earth standing out of the water and in the water:" 6- "Whereby the world that then was, being overflowed with water, perished:" 7- "But the heavens and the earth, which are now, by the same Word are kept in store, reserved unto fire against the day of judgemnt and perdition of ungodly men." And verse 13, "Nevertheless we, according to His promise, look for new heavens and a new earth, wherein dwelleth righeousness."

Now for the iceing on the cake. Look at what the Apostle John wrote in the book of Revelation, chapter 21, verses 1 through 5, "And I saw a new heaven and a new earth: for the first heaven and the first earth were passed away: and there was no more sea." 2- "And I John saw the holy city, new Jeruselem, coming down from God out of heaven,

prepared as a bride adorned for her husband." 3-
"And I heard a great voice out of heaven saying,
Behold, the tabernacle of God is with men, and
He will dwell with them, and they shall be His
people, and God himself shall be with them, and
be their God." 4- "And God shall wipe away all
tears from their eyes; and there shall be no more
death, neither sorrow, nor crying, neither shall
there be any more pain: for the former things
are passed away." 5- "And He that sat upon the
throne said, Behold, I make all things new. And
He said unto me, write: for these words are true
and faithful."

Why Christianity? For me, first and foremost,
I want to be a part of this "new earth" the Bible
speaks of, and to live forever in a place of no pain,
sickness, or suffering of any kind. And I am certain
that God will have much for us to do, and enjoy,
for ages without end.

Is this being selfish and self-centered? Not at
all, it is simply accepting and taking advantage
of what God has to offer in His plan of salvation.
Free, for anyone willing to do the same!

I accept Christianity because of the
overwhelming evidence of God's creation. Along
with the written history of the Bible, the very

orderliness of the universe, and the earth, prove to me that it, and we, were created by an all powerful diety, the God of the Bible. In the Gospel of John, chapter 1, verse 3, "All things were made by Him; and without Him was not anything made that was made."

What is different about this body, that the soul and spirit dwell inside of? Medical science does not have all the answers as to what makes us tick. The human body is a very complex physical and mental entity. Brought into existence from nothing? Impossible! This is one of the biggest lies ever, that Satan has put into the minds of men. The Psalmist penned these words, speaking to God, in Psalm 139:14, "I will praise thee; for I am fearfully and wonderfully made: marvelous are thy works; and that my soul knoweth right well," I just love the last part of this verse,"and <u>that</u> my soul knoweth right well." You see, God has a way of confirming His Word to the human heart that is surrendered to Him.

I accept Christianity because of the prophesy of the written Word. Much of which has already been fulfilled. And it would take another book just to outline what has already taken place. But the exciting thing to me is that we are living in an age of fulfillment. Taking place right before our eyes, at this present time. I understand that this is debateable, however, when current events are compared to Scripture, it appears to be more than just coincidence. Again, this would take another writing to detail what is happening, coinciding with prophesy.

There is a very compelling third reason why I accept Christianity, and probably the most obvious. And that is the existence of Israel as a nation. Is this a surprise to you? Think about it. The Bible is full of her history, from beginning to end. No other nation or people on earth have ever had the Biblical recognition as this minuscule country and her people.

One cannot deny that there is such a place, so why is this of such importance? Because it confirms what God is telling us in His Word, the fulfillment of prophesy right before our eyes! Today, what transpires in Israel effects the entire world. And this is no mis-statement.

All around the world there is hatred brewing over this pint-sized nation. Why is this, if Israel is insignificant? Because Israel continues to be God's chosen people, and He has a "forever" plan for them, regardless if anyone else likes it or not. This information is found in Scripture. And because of the very fact of this nation's existence, I have to believe the Bible is completely and absolutely true in all that it relates to us.

Eternal salvation, by God and through His Son Jesus, is a fact that man can accept or reject. The choice is entirely up to us as an individual. Not coerced by God, but opposed by Satan to deny mankind eternal life. Why Christianity? Because it is reality.

All things near and dear to us will eventually come to an end. We don't especially Iike to face this fact, but that's life, and death; the thing people find most difficult to think about. This is the big reason so many people are "infatuated," and I use that word on purpose, with "health care." One of the biggest political subjects being debated and discussed in the country these days.

We will do <u>anything</u> to prolong the life of this mortal body, yet have no real concern for our undying soul. Human life is short, and we should do the right things to maintain a healthy body. The bible tells us how to do this also, but without the worry that we may fall apart physically. Yes, medical science has come a long way, but it cannot cure the fear of sickness and death.

Why Christianity? Because only God can alleviate and take away from our mind the fear factor. Eternity is without measure, and our soul is eternal, so , what have you done to care for this most priceless part of your existence?

Real Christians do not get whipped up into a frenzy to riot and cause destruction just because someone insulted or ridiculed Christ or Christianity. This simply does not happen among true believers. There is <u>only</u> one way, and the assurance to be gained is without measure.

Chapter Eleven

What Will It Take?

The title of this chapter is a broad question, but the one I want to discuss is, what will it take to be a real Christian? I am not talking about a title one would assume merely to be part of a group; or pretend to be something you are not. That, of course, would be hypocrisy. But many are guilty of that very thing. And this is the excuse used by a lot of folks for not attending church, they don't want to associate with a bunh of hypocrits. Although, before you can find a counterfeit, there has to be "the real thing."

There are those who claim to be followers of Christ for a number of reasons. One would be for personal, or monetary gain, to impress a church congregation as being one of them. Another reason is that it just seems to be the right thing to do, but a change of heart and life-style never really takes place. A third reason would be to sow discord among true believers. This is Satan driven and it happens frequently.

What are the criteria of a true Christian? In other words, how does one differentiate between a "believer" and a "non-believer?" Perhaps you have never thought of it in this way, but there are certain standards that must be followed. These established rules are not man made, but are ordained of God. Is it not rational judgment for a created mortal being to receive directions from our immortal Creator? This is a major hurdle for many people to get over.

The Bible is very clear as to what must be done to become a Christian. First , we must recognize the fact that every individual is a sinner, and should be reconciled to a Holy God. This is the first step of repentance. We all start out in the same boat. Rich man, poor man, bond man, or free, every one is spiritually dead until they accept the gift that God has provided through His Son, Christ Jesus. And the beautiful thing is, this decision is completely voluntary, not forced by God or anyone else. A willful surrendering of one's life to God, and <u>living</u> for Him until we die, and then, for eternity. Oh yes, at some point in time, everyone will have to make this decision.

Repentance is complete when we recognize our sin, confess to God of our guilt, ask for His forgiveness, accept it by faith, and live a <u>changed</u>, or righteous life, by following the directions found in the Bible. And "following the directions" is always the highest hurdle. You can argue against this simple analysis until you are blue in the face, but it will not change the process that God has set forth, or the requirements He demands of all who would follow Him.

There is a great amount of Scripture concerning this matter, however, I will use only a few verses to make my point. Romans 3: 22 and 23, "Even the righteousness of God, which is by faith of Jesus Christ unto all and upon all them that believe: for there is no difference:" 23- "For all have sinned, and come short of the glory of God."

First John 3:8, "He that commiteth sin is of the devil; for the devil sinneth from the beginning.

For this purpose the Son of God was manifested, that He might destroy the works of the devil."

Because of the fact that we are all sinners, God, in His mercy and grace, provided His Son to be our redeemer. You can also argue the point that not all have been given the opportunity to hear the Gospel message, or Good News, of redemption. But, because God is all wise, and knowing the hearts of every individual, it is the Holy Spirit, the third person of the Trinity, who takes care of this matter. Remember the "conscience" we were born with? And I believe there is a time of accountability when we can descern between right and wrong.

In the Gospel of John, chapter 6, verse 44, Jesus had this to say, "No man can come to me, except the Father which hath sent me draw him: and I will raise him up at the last day."

Ephesians, chapter 2, verses 18 and 22, "For through Him (Jesus) we both have access by one Spirit unto the Father." 22- "In whom ye (believers) also are builded together for an habitation of God through the Spirit."

This is the spiritual re-birth of our soul, which will gain us entry into Heaven, and what God has prepared for those who commit to Him.

As was already stated, acknowledging our standing before God as a sinner, is only the first step of repentance, we will dig a little deeper into the "how to" aspect of this act. Repentance is being sorry for bad deeds we have commited. Some will repent when they are caught doing something wrong, but will have no remorse for the actual perpetration. When there is no true sorrow over a sin we have commited, there is no real repentance.

It is an emotional sense of regret over our past actions. We become conscience stricken about things we have done that we know were not right. There's that word "conscience" again! And finally, it is deep felt sorrow for wrong- doing, or for sins we have commited, that brings about a change of life, and how we think. A desire to please God and live for Him. Jesus tells us in Luke 13:3, the last part of the verse, "…….except ye repent , ye shall all likewise perish." And, we read in the book of Acts, chapter 3, verse 19, "Repent ye therefore, and be converted, that your sins may be blotted out, when the times of refreshing shall come from the presence of the Lord." Now we will go to chapter 17 of this same book, verses 29 and 30, "Forasmuch then, as we are the offspring of God, we ought not to think that the Godhead is like unto gold, or silver, or stone graven by art and mans device." 30- "And the times of this ignorance God winked at; but now commandeth all men every where to repent:"

The act of repentance is not a matter of choice, if one is to become a Christian, it is a <u>command</u> of God. The matter of choice comes in when we decide to choose, or reject, the plan of salvation that God has freely offered to everyone. We can think of repentance as the beginning, or the embryonic stage, of Christianity.

For the true believer there will come what I refer to as a "remodeling" of our life style. If there is no make-over from our worldly habits and living, into a "new" life of righteousness, how could we be accepted by God as one of His children?

To begin our change of life, we must deal with "confession." This is a personal matter between an individual and God, not another person. The need to confess a wrong-doing against our fellow man comes under a different category. To God, <u>all</u> wrong-doing is sin, regarless of what classification given by man; if it is a "little" sin or a "big" sin.

We will get right into our Scripture references on this subject, beginning with Proverbs 28:13, "He that covereth his sins shall not prosper: but whoso confesseth and forsaketh them shall have mercy." I am using this particular verse for a specific reason. In this world there are many unsavory and wicked people who prosper abundantly in material wealth. And many people, and especially new Christians wonder, why? Christianity has to do with our spiritual man, not the mortal. When one accepts Jesus as Savior and Lord, they must direct their life toward an <u>eternal</u> prosperity! Now, don't get me wrong, I have nothing what-so-ever against wealth. Money is a necessary thing that is required in order to meet our daily needs. I would like all Christians to prosper <u>abundantly</u> in their finances! This would be a real boon to the cause of spreading the Gospel message.

Now, back to our subject. We must first make our confession to God, who has the power of forgiveness. Then, as a Christian, we must be ready to confess our belief in God to anyone who would question our faith, or wonder why we are "different." Romans, chapter 10, verses 9 and 10, will get us off to a good start, "That if thou shalt confess with thy mouth the Lord Jesus, and shalt believe in thine heart that God hath raised Him from the dead, thou shalt be saved." 10- "For with the heart man believeth unto righteousness; and with the mouth confession is made unto salvation."

First John 1:9, "If we confess our sins, He is faithful and just to forgive us our sins, and to cleanse us from all unrighteousness." Now we go to chapter 4 of this same book, verse 2, "Hereby know ye the Spirit of God: every spirit that confesseth that Jesus Christ is come in the flesh is of God."

We have to acknowledge Christ for who He says He is. That He is the Son of God, born as a man to understand our human weakness. And to be an example for us to follow. Without becoming a man of human flesh, He could not die for our sin, nor could He suffer the pain of humanity in order to be the sacrifice for our sin. And, the Holy Spirit will confirm to our spirit that we <u>are</u> a partaker of God's gift of salvation.

Then, we have this assurance from Christ Himself, found in Matthew 10:32, "Whosoever therefore shall confess Me before men, him will I confess also before my Father which is in heaven."

Another facet of a true Christian is "belief." And this is also where faith comes in. Believing, is a confidence, and conviction, of the doctrine set forth in the Bible. That it is the <u>true</u> and <u>infallible</u> Word of God.

The Gospel of John 20:31, "But these are written that ye might believe that Jesus is the Christ, the Son of God; and that believing ye might have life through His name."

The book of Acts, chapter 13, verse 39, "And by Him all that believe are justified from all things, from which ye could not be justified by the law of Moses."

It is my firm belief that the Bible was written for the specific purpose of introducing the Son of God to mankind for our redemption, or salvation, from eternal punishment. Hebrews 10:39, "But we are not of them who draw back unto perdition; but of them that believe to the saving of the soul."

Now we come to the faith aspect of our belief. The Bible gives us the definition of faith in Hebrews 11:1, "Now faith is the substance of things hoped for, the evidence of things not seen." The dictionary version of faith is: Unquestioning belief that does not require proof or evidence. At first glance there seems to be little contradiction in these two explanations of faith. Since faith is intangible and cannot be seen with the human eye, it does take an unquestioning belief in something or someone. The Bible tells us that faith is the substance, or reality of things hoped for, and the evidence, or proof, of things not seen. Now "substance," "evidence" and "things," are all tangible and verifiable. This is what faith in God will accomplish, the reality and proof of His existence. The faith we are discussing here is not some dream of material gain, but a soul saving faith that leads to eternal life, and that will be the reality and the proof of our faith in Christ.

Galatians 3:22, "But the Scripture hath concluded all under sin, that the promise by faith of Jesus Christ might be given to them that believe."

Romans 1: 16 and 17, "For I am not ashamed of the gospel of Christ: for it is the power of God unto salvation to every one that believeth; to the Jew first, and also to the Greek." 17- "For therein is the righteousness of God revealed from faith to faith: as it is written, The just shall live by faith."

The next item on our to-do list, of becoming a Christian, is "acceptance." And this is a two -way street, between man and God. When we accept God at His Word, He will accept us into His eternal fellowship, or salvation, of true believers.

First, we must accept the "gift" that God has offered, and provided through His Son. A gift is something that is offered to show love or affection, friendship and favor. But in order to receive a gift that is offered, we must accept this gift <u>willingly</u>. The Gift of God is the sacrifice of His Son for our redemption. Romans 6:23, "For the wages of sin is death; but the gift of God is eternal life through Jesus Christ our Lord." Second Corinthians 9:15, "Thanks be unto God for His unspeakable gift."

An "unspeakable gift" is one that is marvelous, awesome, one that cannot be spoken because it is beyond human expression, as to defy description. And this is simply the dictionary meaning. But it is truth, because we cannot put into words exactly what it means to receive such a magnanimous gift. However, this is just the beginning, because we are given this assurance in James 1:17, "Every good gift and every perfect gift is from above, and cometh down from the Father of lights, with whom is no variableness, neither shadow of turning." And here is one of my favorite verses of Scripture, First Corinthians 2:9, "But as it is written, Eye hath not seen, nor ear heard, neither have entered into the heart of man, the things which God hath prepared for them that love Him."

There is one thing we can be absolutely sure of, and that is, God does not change on a whim. He is not capricious, but steadfast and reliable. He is our rock to lean upon!

Hebrews 12: 28 and 29, "Wherefore we receiving a kingdom which cannot be moved, let us have grace, whereby we may serve God acceptably with reverence and Godly fear:" 29- "For our God is a consuming fire."

When we accept Christ as our savior and Lord, it means that we agree to His terms, or commandments, whereby we revere God and recognize His authority over our life, that we may serve Him out of love and respect. In reference to that 29th verse, we go to the Old Testament book of Deuteronomy, chapter 4, verse 24, "For the Lord thy God is a consuming fire, even a jealous God."

This could easily be misunderstood about the "consuming fire" and the "jealous God" statements. Since we are the creation of God, made to have fellowship with Him, He is greatly concerned about our welfare. Concerned enough to sacrifice His Son for our sake. And He will jealously guard us from the attacks of Satan, if we allow Him to do so, by turning to Him for guidance. God will devastate our adversaries if we trust in Him.

In the 19th Psalm, verse 14, the Psalmist writes this, "Let the words of my mouth, and the meditation of my heart, be acceptable in thy sight , O Lord, my strength and my redeemer." This should be our prayer also! To sum up our thought, we read Acts 10:35, "But in every nation he that feareth Him, and worketh righteousness, is accepted with Him."

"Commitment" is also on our list of things to do. The dictionary meaning of the word "commit" helps us understand our ability to actually put our faith into action. Quote- "To give in charge or trust; to deliver for safe -keeping; entrust; consign. To hand over or set apart to be disposed of or put to some purpose." End of quote.

When we commit our life to Christ, we give Him charge, or the responsibility and duty, to take control of our thoughts and activities. We entrust, or invest, our time for Him. We are to be set apart for His purpose. And in doing all of this, our soul will be in safe keeping for eternity. Now I ask this question, for you to think about, since eternity is forever, is our commitment to God worth the effort? You decide.

Psalm 37: 3 through 5, "Trust in the Lotrd, and do good; so shalt thou dwell in the land, and verily thou shalt be fed." 4- "Delight thyself also in the Lord; and He shall give thee the desires of thine heart." 5- "Commit thy way unto the Lord; trust also in Him; and He shall bring it to pass."

I am fully aware of why many look at this Scripture with skepticism. In times past, I also have said, "Lord, you haven't given me the desires of my heart, why is this?"

After much self-examination, I had to ask myself some hard questions. How strong and commited is my trust in God? Do I really give Him charge of my life, or am I holding back in areas that I want to control? Then the most troubling question came to mind, do I actually delight myself in the Lord? This demanded some very serious introspection on my part. Do I find joy and happiness in living for God? Is He the source of my pleasure and contentment? These are all good questions, and must be answered before we accuse the Lord of not meeting the desires of our heart.

If we meet the acceptable criteria, just possibly, the desires of our heart may not be for our own good, or to fulfill <u>His</u> will for our life. After all is said and done, we are facing eternity, so what shall we do, go our way or God's way? Commitment is where the rubber meets the road. It is a reality check of our sincerity.

This is another two-way street between God and mankind. Before we ever commit to God, He has already made a commitment to us. Second Corinthians 5:19, "To wit, that God was in Christ, reconciling the world unto Himself, not imputing their trespasses unto them; and hath commited unto us the word of reconciliation."

This verse says it all; God, through His Son, Jesus Christ, made a way of forgiveness so we would not have to bear our own sin, but can be reconciled to God through His plan of salvation.

This brings us to our final item on the list of what it takes to be a Christian, and that is, "living the life." First, let me clear up another matter. It is not a set rule that the afore mentioned items, confession, believing, acceptance, and commitment, come in that order. They could all happen simultaneously, or over a period of time. God works in each individual as His truth becomes clear in our mind. But they are all necessary requirements in order to "live the life" of a Christian.

That old saying, "the proof is in the pudding," applies here. If there is a real change of heart from the old man of sin into a person of righteousness, our life-style will be different, prior to conversion. It is no longer the "same-old, same-old" way of doing things. Our life becomes new and with a different purpose. Brought about by a spiritual re-birth, or regeneration. Our soul, which was dead in trespasses and sin, and headed for eternal death, is now reconciled to God through Christ unto eternal life.

Ephesians, chapter 4, verses 22 through 24, gives us a starting point for our new way of living, "That ye put off concerning the former conversation the old man, which is corrupt according to the deceitful lusts;" 23- "And be renewed in the spirit of your mind;" 24- "And that ye put on the new man, which after God is created in righteousness and true holiness."

Two distinct things happen at conversion. The thoughts of our mind change, and the purpose of our life changes. A spiritual change brings about a physical, or life-style change. In the Gospel of John, chapter 3, verses 3 and 6, Jesus had this to say, ".......,Verily, verily, I say unto thee, except a man be born again, he cannot see the kingdom of

God." 6- "That which is born of the flesh is flesh, and that which is born of the Spirit is spirit."

Now the question arises, what brings about a renewing of the mind and a spirirual rebirth? We will go back to the Old Testament to see what it takes to qualify. Deuteronomy 6:5, "And thou shalt love the Lord thy God with all thine heart, and with all thy soul, and with all thy might."

This commandment is repeated in the New Testament, and taken one step further when Jesus spoke these words, Mark 12: 30 and 31, "And thou shalt love the Lord thy God with all thy heart, and with all thy soul, and with all thy mind, and with all thy strength: this is the first commandment." 31- "And the second is like, namely this, Thou shalt love thy neighbor as thyself. There is none other commandment greater than these."

Jesus brings emphasis to this second commandment in John 13:34, "A new commandment I give unto you, That ye love one another; as I have loved you, that ye also love one another." Talk about something that will bring change to one's life! When we start loving God as we are supposed to do, and go beyond that to include our brothers, our neighbors, and one another, it kind of gets down to the realization of what Christianity is all about.

It would be well to consider what the Apostle Paul wrote to the Christians at Galatia. Galatians 2:20, "I am crucified with Christ: nevertheless I live; yet not I, but Christ liveth in me: and the life which I now live in the flesh I live by the faith of the Son of God, who loved me, and gave Himself for me."

Paul wrote almost the same thing to the church at Philippi, only in a more concise statement: Philippians 1:21, "For to me to live is Christ, and to die is gain."

The Apostle Paul understood exactly what it means to live a Christian life. This brings us back to the commandments we were given, to love God with all of our being, and our neighbor as ourself, does it not? How we live has everything to do with being a Christian. In Matthew 4:4, when Jesus was tempted by Satan, we find this response, "But He answered and said, It is written, Man shall not live by bread alone, but by every word that proceedeth out of the mouth of God." In the book of First Peter, chapter 1: verse 23, the Apostle wrote this, "Being born again, not of corruptible seed, but of incorruptible, by the Word of God, which liveth and abideth forever."

So, what do we glean from all of this? First and foremost is to recognize our subservience to the Almighty God of the Bible, the Creator of the heavens and the earth. That our main purpose in life is to please Him, in whatever capacity He chooses. First Peter 1:18 and 19, "For as much as ye know that ye were not redeemed with corruptible things, as silver and gold, from your vain conversation received by tradition from your fathers;" 19- "But with the precious blood of Christ, as of a lamb without blemish and without spot:" First Corinthians 6:20, "For ye were bought with a price: therefore glorify God in your body, and in your spirit, which are God's." The carnal mind does not understand what it means to glorify God in our body and our spirit. It is a spiritual transformation that takes place, converting a non-believer into a believer and follower of Christ.

Secondly, it is a life long walk, one day at a time, seeking God's devine direction in <u>all</u> that we do or think. At every opportunity sharing the Good News of the Gospel to those who do not realize that eternity is in the balance. Conversion is instantaneous, it takes place the moment one accepts Christ as their Savior. However, it is a "growing up," or maturing process that continues within us until the end of life. First Peter 2: 2 and 3, "As newborn babes, desire the sincere milk of the Word, that ye may grow thereby:" 3- "If so be ye have tasted that the Lord is gracious."

And thirdly, Christianity is definitely not for wimps and losers! However, it is through the power of God, and our faith in Him and what He has promised, that makes it all possible and worthwhile.

"Forever" is a long time. Have you considered <u>where</u> you want to spend it?

Chapter Twelve

An Elusive Dream

In this book, I have brought up a number of issues, all dealing with character, attitude, and the way we live. Things that will determine our eternal destiny.

The meaning of words, and how they can be used to either harm or build up, depending upon the purpose for which they are used. It was brought up that there is an on-going "war of words" between opposing ideologies in this country that goes so far as to spark physical codfrontation. And the rhetoric intensifies when it becomes an issue of good verses evil.

The meaning of martyrdom and how it is being falsely portrayed by those whose only ambition is world domination. Simply twisting the meaning of a word to justify an evil doctrine.

Next was discussed the "wellness" of America. The deterioration of our morality, our strength and our wealth. How these three areas are intertwined to impact the health of this country. As we become more dependant upon government for our every need, we degrade into a weaker society and less able to function on our own.

Then we talked about the spiritual, or moral condition we have arrived at. And how this is the root cause of all the other illness besetting this nation. God has been brought down to the level of mortal man, or rejected altogether. One being just as bad as the other. How our government passes laws in complete contradiction to God's commandments, and how we viewed them in days gone by. This is a true measure of our morality, or lack of any resemblance of what is good.

We discussed the road that most people are traveling, and the road that is less traveled. Also the direction and final destination of each way.

Then came the topic of "why Christianity?" And what does it mean to be a Christian? I have gone through a number of subjects, however, these last two thoughts are the more relevant of any, because eternity is the bottom line of all this discussion.

You see, I believe that most people view life through a hazy perspective. Not wanting to accept the fact that it is terminal. I have quoted Scripture a great deal in this writing, and some have been repeated for a reason. So, if you don't mind, I will repeat Hebrews 9:27, "And as it is appointed unto men once to die, but after this the judgment."

No one is going to miss this arrangement to meet our maker, stand before Him and give an account of how we lived our life.

I gave reference to different individuals who acquired a certain amount of fame and worldly prominence. Most died at a young age by other than natural causes. They had one thing in common, and it is the same with multitudes of people, they were following an "elusive dream." To a certain degree this holds true for all of us.

Young people are constantly told to seek a goal in life and work towards that end. Many of these goals are dreams of wealth and fame, or success in whatever occupation they choose. To some it ia a struggle to arrive at their "elusive dream," never accheving real happiness or satisfaction, even though they appear to have accomplished above average success.

I will be so bold to say that everyone <u>needs</u> a purpose in life. And I will ask the question, to what end will our intention, or determination, bring us?

Do you suppose that those famous people I mentioned, who died of an alcohol or drug induced death, by suicide, or being killed, thought of ending their mortal life in this manner? Or was this the result of an elusive dream they were following?

Yes, there is a certain amount of satisfaction in accomplishing our dreams and goals, but more ofen than not, they have no eternal value.

Now we arrive at the crux of the matter, the deciding point; the choice I will make. Do I decide on life or death? Oh you say, everyone wants to choose life! You see, in our mortal life we choose our immortal destiny. Do I choose God's way , or the ways of the world, which is Satans way?

As a guide to travel the right road, the straight and narrow one, we find this advice in the book of Colossians, chapter 3, verse 2, "Set your affection on things above, not on things on the earth."

Now, before you accuse me of living in some kind of nether land of mythology or mysticism, I want you to know that Christianity, as defined in the Bible, is reality!

Christians live their life as anyone else, by the fact that they provide sustenance, or a means of livelihood, for themselves and their families. In other words, we live in the world, but at the same time, by the grace of God, try not to succumb to the temptations of the world that are contrary to His commandments. Refrain from taking part in unGodly activities, and anything that has the appearance of being evil.

A true Christian does not engage in subterfuge or deception to hide their faith in God, and what it means to them. Let us review again what it says in Colossians 2: 8 through 10, in the NIV translation, "See to it that no one takes you captive through hollow and deceptive philosophy, which depends on human tradition and the basic principles of this world rather than on Christ." 9- "For in Christ all the fullness of the Diety lives in bodily form," 10- "And you have been given fullness in Christ, who is the head over every power and authority."

I have heard the derision many times that it is boring and no fun to go to church, or believe in the Bible. It cramps one's life-style and "I want to live life to the fullest," is the mantra of the worldly minded person. Not even considering that there is coming a day of reckoning. You can have all the "fun" you so desire, but it is only an elusive dream, with no value whatsoever in eternity. When we persue the lusts of the flesh, we become blind to what is righteous and fail to see beyond this mortal life.

In chapter eleven of this book, the question was asked, what will it take to be a Christian? After counting the cost, and considering the pros and cons, I came to the conclusion that it will take our "life." A life surrendered to the will of God. An impossibility for those who think Christianity is for wimps and losers.

Most of us will not be required to do great and mighty works for God, but we will be held responsible for what we know to do. James 4:17, "Therefore to him that knoweth to do good, and doeth it not, to him it is sin."

First Timothy 6:12, "Fight the good fight of faith, lay hold on eternal life, whereunto thou art also called, and hast professed a good profession before many witnesses." We are called to be witnesses for Christ, by the life we live and the things we say and do. This brings to mind again the real martyrs. Just what did they have that they could face death rather than renounce their belief in Christ? Good question! In my mind, I would venture to say that they had a clear picture of eternity. They knew without a doubt that where they were going was not worth a temporary extention of their physical, or mortal life. Does this appear wimp-like to you?

There will be no wimps in Heaven because they are the ones without the backbone to do what is right. Or the self-righteous who look to their "good works" as being enough to get there. Or those who justify their life by believing that a merciful God does not send people to hell, or eternal punishment. It is true that God does not "send" anyone there, it is a decision that is made by a person's unbelief and rejection of God's gift of salvation.

In the Gospels of Matthew 9:13, Mark 2:17, and Luke 5:32, Jesus said, "I came not to call the righteous, but sinners to repentance." Romans 3:10, "As it is written, There is none righteous, no, not one:" Christ died to save sinners, which includes everyone. Jesus wants us to come to Him, with all the warts and blemishes of sin in our life, to receive mercy and forgiveness.

There will be no wimps in Heaven because it takes the right attitude to acknowledge our need of cleansing from sin.

The heady and high-minded just don't cut it. It cannot be an "only me" mind-set, because God is no respector of persons. There must be an understanding of His Lordship, and the desire to please Him. People who are impetuous, haughty, proud, and arrogant, don't like the idea of being subservient, or submissive unto God, even though we are His creation. In spite of the false claims of those who preach evolution..

A doubtful person does not qualify for Heaven because they are uncertain, always questioning what the Bible teaches.

Never able to arrive at an absolute sureness of what is right or wrong. Skeptical that Christianity is the "only" way. Hebrews 3:14, "For we are made partakers of Christ, if we hold the beginning of our confidence stedfast unto the end;"

There is no turning back from following Christ if we maintain the confidence we found in Him when we first believed, until the time we die. Salvation is not a "feel good" experience, it is a good feeling <u>knowing</u> that Jesus is with us unto the end of this life and <u>beyond</u>!

A person that believes there are numerous ways to Heaven are also unqualified. They simply reject God's Word and condemn themselves to eternal damnation. To many this may seem harsh and cruel, but Holy Scripture teaches that there is <u>only one way</u>, and that is through Jesus Christ.

Wealth and fame are not a ticket to Heaven. In fact, in most cases, they are a stumbling block, causing one to lose sight of what is righteous and pure in God's eyes.

There will be no wimps in Heaven because wimps do not have the courage to stand up to Satan when faced with ridicule, intimidation, and the threat of death. When so-called "friends" laugh at you for going to church and making an attempt to clean up your life. Who mock you and become angry because they have no more influence over you. Threats of bodily harm are certainly not easy to face, but they may come. If one had to look death square in the eye because of their belief in Christ, what would you do? Many face this choice today, in what we call a day of "enlightenment" and "tolerance." Satan will not enlighten anyone and he will not tolerate losing a follower without a fight.

Choices must be made that will decide if we have what it takes. In the 68th Psalm, verse 20, we are told this, "He that is our God is the God of salvation; and unto God the Lord belong the issues from death." And in Proverbs 4:23, we are given this instruction, "Keep thy heart with all diligence; for out of it are the issues of life." In plain words, our <u>choices</u> are a matter of life or death, in eternity.

Have you ever considered the meaning of the word "issue?" Just what are these issues we have to face? These "issues from death," and "the issues of life," and just how important are they?

The dictionary gives a rather long and complex meaning to the word "issue." The first rendering is an exit, or a means of going out, an outlet. The next is a result or consquence. To be born, to accrue, to enter into conflict. This is only a brief summary of this seemingly innocent word.

However, they all apply to what Scripture is trying to tell us. When we deal with the "issues from death," is there an actual exit, or a means of going out of this state of being? And what is the consquence or result of death?

What about "the issues of life?" We are born into this world, we grow physically, we accrue possessions, either few or in quantity. However, no one escapes the conflicts of life.

The Bible tells us that we have to deal with all of these questions and circumstances. What many do not understand is, these matters are more than simply "here an now" mortal concerns. They are also spiritual, having to do with eternity. This is what separates the true believer from the phony and the non-believer. I mean a belief in God, through Christ, our redeemer, that we live by on a daily basis, come what may!

This mortal life is a preparation place for eternity. If not taken care of in the "here and now," there will be no second chance. I am not judging anyone, only pointing out what God is telling us in His Word. The very reason He sent His Son to die for mankind.

God has provided a remedy for the issues of life and death, and it is called "salvation." It is for anyone, and everyone who chooses to accept this free gift. The catch is, we must meet His requirements. First Corinthians 6: 19 and 20, gives light to this matter, "What? Know ye not that your body is the temple of the Holy Ghost which is in you, which ye have of God, and ye are not your own?" 20- "For ye are bought with a price: therefore glorify God in your body, and in your spirit, which are God's."

Every person on the face of this planet belongs to God. However, He has put within us the ability to choose or reject Him. In order to attain salvation, we must willingly accept the commitment to follow Jesus. In either case, to become a follower, or not, God has already decided our eternal destiny, it is by our own choice. In other words, God has two places prepared for eternity and we get to take our pick. It is not His will if one chooses to perish, but our own decision because of rejection.

Second Peter 3:9, "The Lord is not slack concerning His promise, as some men count slackness; but is longsuffering to us-ward, not willing that any should perish, but that all should come to repentance." There you have it in a few words. It takes repentance, with a change of heart and living for God, to make it into Heaven.

If you believe that this is overly simple, I challenge you to try it. What a person thinks they have to give up in this life to follow Christ, does not compare with what they will gain in eternity with Him.

To those who accuse Christians of being wimps and losers, please answer these questions: What do you have to offer that is better? Why do you hate what is good? Why is your mind closed to the truth? What are you afraid of? Do you ignore your conscience? What true Christian has done you any harm? And what will you say when you stand before God?

Many more questions could be asked, but it would be pointless to those who desire evil things rather than righteousness. Life is a battle between good and evil, no doubt about it. However, those that choose good have God on their side, and in the end, will gain victory over evil. Psalm 53:1, "The fool hath said in his heart, There is no God. Corrupt are they, and have done abominable iniquity: there is none that doeth good." This may be considered a very harsh verse of Scripture, comparing those who deny God to a fool. Without God, no one is good, and they do terrible and hateful things. Many just follow the crowd and go along with the world, not taking into account the consequences of their words and deeds.

As for the Christian, we find great strength in Scripture, such as Romans 8:31, "What shall we then say to these things? If God be for us, who can be against us?"

Strange as it may seem to the unbeliever, it makes no difference what we must face in life, when we have Christ on our side. Personally, I cannot imagine a day going by without knowing that I can call on God for help and guidance. Circumstances may at times be very difficult, but God will never leave us nor forsake us. In my own life this has proven to be true. Looking back, I can see that it was the hand of God intervening on my behalf more times than not. You might say that it was only coincidence, or simply happenstance, that made things seem to work out. When God brings about a result, it is not accidental or mere chance. In my case, I am talking about many years of events that <u>only</u> God could casuse to happen.

This is what makes our faith strong, when we can recognize the hand of God as we face adversity and uncertainty. Do I have what it takes to be a Christian? Not on my own strength! But I do know <u>what</u> I believe, and <u>in whom</u> I believe! That much is clear in my mind. You have to experience this type of assurance to know what I am talking about. And this is certainly <u>not</u> self-righteousness, but the confidence we find in God's infallible

Word, the Bible, plus the inner peace that is found nowhere else.

I realize that not everyone will agree with my line of reasoning. However, as I witness all of the turmoil and hatred in the world, I know that there is a better way of life. I have found this "better way" through Christ, who gave His very life for me, But not only me! I have read and studied other "religions" and philosophies, and none can compare to what true Christianity really means. A guarantee of eternal life, and I will take God's Word on this over what anyone says to the contrary. Jesus is my confidence!

There will be no wimps in Heaven because the criteria for entrance is very straight and narrow, and not many will choose it.

I must address one thing I have not stressed enough. While we are in this life, preparing for the next one, does not mean that Christians are not up-beat people. Just the opposite, we are the happiest people on earth, believe it or not. In the midst of sin and all sorts of evil, the ray of hope in Christ shines brighter every day. Our hope is not in this world, or of the government taking care of us, but our hope is eternal, based on the promises found in God's Word. <u>Real</u> joy and peace of mind come from God!

Christianity is reality, as I have already mentioned. Material wealth, and all this world has to offer, is only temporary and short lived at best. The grim reaper is going to call only on those without hope of eternity. For the Christian, passing from this life to the next is just the beginning of a blessed <u>everlasting</u> life. What a marvelous day that will be! My hope in Christ is a change from mortality into immortality. What better hope is there? It is certainly an eternity better than the alternitive. And this is definitely not an elusive dream!

In the book of Second Timothy, chapter 3, verses 2 through5, we are given a list of appalling and sinful behavior, "For men shall be lovers of their own selves, covetous, boasters, proud, blasphemers, disobedient to parents, unthankful, unholy," 3- "Without natural affection, trucebreakers, false accusers, incontinent, fierce, despisers of those that are good," 4- "Traitors, heady, highminded, lovers of pleasures more than lovers of God;" 5- "Having a form of godliness, but denying the power thereof: from such turn away."

In all of these areas listed above, we find the meaning of the word "wimp." Weak, ineffectual, and insipid. Without repentance, none of these will make it into Heaven. Without question, there will be no wimps in Heaven because they all reject and disbelieve in the only way to get there. How sad.

John 3:16, "For God so loved the world, that He gave His only begotten Son, that whosoever believeth in Him should not perish, but have everlasting life."

This natural life is so short and uncertain, that to not accept Christ as Savior and Lord is beyond comprehension. Yes, I realize that this statement will be called radical and far-fetched by all worldly minded thinkers. But what is their answer, or solution, for eternity? To simply ignore and reject the idea and it will go away? Something deep within our conscience makes us aware of the truth of an "after life." A person may deny the reality of eternal life with all the gusto they can muster, however, they are only fooling themselves.

I must be very clear as to the reason why this is so important. The Spirit of God will not always try to convince an individual to repent, so it is vital that we understand this. Genesis 6: the first part of verse 3, (NIV translation) "Then the Lord said, My Spirit will not contend with man foever, for he is mortal,......." And in Romans 1:28, (NIV) "Furthermore, since they did not think it worthwhile to retain the knowledge of God, He gave them over to a depraved mind, to do what ought not to be done."

Now, let's get to the basis of why and how this happens. Proverbs 1:7, (NIV) "The fear of the Lord is the beginning of knowledge: but fools despise wisdom and discipline." Next, we go to verses 24 through 31, "But since you rejected me when I called and no one gave heed when I stretched out my hand," 25- "Since you ignored all my advice and would not accept my rebuke," 26- "I in turn will laugh at your disaster; I will mock when calamity overtakes you." 27- "When calamity overtakes you like a storm, when disaster sweeps over you like a whirlwind, when distress and trouble overwhelm you." 28- "Then they will call to me but I will not answer; they will look for me but will not find me." 29- "Since they hated knowledge and did not choose to fear the Lord," 30- "Since they would not accept my advice and spurned my rebuke,"

31- "They will eat the fruit of their ways and be filled with the fruit of their schemes."

When a person becomes obsessed with their own plans and schemes, and reject what God has offered, it will bring about dire consequences, and God will not hear them in their time of calamity.

How serious is this? Second Thessalonians 2:12 answers this question, "That they all might be damned who believed not the truth, but had pleasure in unrighteousness."

Have you ever considered the word "damned?" The very simple meaning is this: "Condemned or <u>deserving</u> condemnation - souls doomed to eternal punishment." Not at all pleasant to think about, and the very reason many will turn away from Biblical instruction.

So, what is the root cause of damnation? What did we read in Romans 1:28? They did not like to retain God in their knowledge! They chose the easy, worldly way of living, giving no heed to righteousness. Utterly refusing the grace and forgiveness that God offered through His Son. God gave them over to a reprobate mind, to do those things which were evil. The rest of the chapter goes on to list a multitude of "things" people do that are unacceptable to God, causing their eternal destruction.

Titus 1:16, "They profess that they know God; but in works they deny Him, being abominable, and disobedient, and unto every good work reprobate."

Second Timothy 3:7, "Ever learning, and never able to come to the knowledge of the truth."

At the end of this game of life, there is no excuse we can give to escape damnation if we have continually rejected the truth of God's Word. John 12:48, Jesus speaking, "He that rejecteth me, and receiveth not my words, hath one that judgeth him: the word that I have spoken, the same shall judge him in the last day."

I have made reference to much Scripture in this narrative, and even repeated some. But it is this very Word of God that will be our judge into eternity. To reject this Word will bring damnation, to accept it will bring everlasting life.

There will be no wimps in Heaven because they choose to go down the "broad road" that leads to destruction; by their own volition, with no one to blame but themselves.

I will conclude my Scripture references with this final verse, Second Corinthians 13:5,

"Examine yourselves, whether ye be in the faith; prove your own selves. Know ye not your own selves, how that Jesus Christ is in you, except ye be reprobates?"

Without Christ we <u>are</u> reprobate; depraved, corrupt, unprincipled, excluded from salvation and lost in sin. Not a good situation, to say the least.

This journey through life is really a race against time, because we don't kmow when it will end. The most important question is, have we done what it takes to ensure our rightful place in eternity? It is a decision that every person will make, either willingly, or by forfiture through unbelief. It is a life or death responsibility of a personal nature, and what one chooses will determine their destiny. It will take courage, perseverance, and the will to win, that will activate our faith in God to see us through to everlasting life.

Thank God for the remedy that He has provided through His Son, for <u>whosoever</u> chooses to believe! And there will be no wimps in Heaven!

www.ingramcontent.com/pod-product-compliance
Lightning Source LLC
Chambersburg PA
CBHW030258290526
45785CB00001B/138